Joan Baez

Singer With a Cause

by Jeffrey Heller

CHILDRENS PRESS®
CHICAGO

.₂ ₍ ¹ ₂

01032 8192

ACKNOWLEDGMENTS

The editors would like to acknowledge use of excerpted material from the following works:

"Joan Baez" by Make Sager from *Rolling Stone Magazine*, November 15, 1987. By Straight Arrow Publishers, Inc. © 1987. All Rights Reserved. Reprinted by Permission.

"Joan Baez: The Rolling Stone Interview" by Kurt Loder from *Rolling Stone Magazine*, April 14, 1983. By Straight Arrow Publishers, Inc. © 1983. All Rights Reserved. Reprinted by Permission.

"The 100 Best Singles of the Last 25 Years" from *Rolling Stone Magazine*, September 8, 1988. By Straight Arrow Publishers, Inc. © 1988. All Rights Reserved. Reprinted by Permission.

"Summer's Gain, Autumn's Loss," published in August 23, 1969 issue of *Saturday Review*. Reprinted by permission.

Courtesy *Mademoiselle*. Copyright © 1964 by The Conde Nast Publications Inc.

Copyright 1962 Time Inc. All rights reserved. Reprinted by permission from TIME.

Reprinted from *Philadelphia Daily News*. Copyright © 1985. Used by permission.

AND A VOICE TO SING WITH by Joan Baez. Copyright © 1987 by Joan Baez. Reprinted by permission of Summit Books, a division of Simon Schuster, Inc.

"Children of the Eighties" by Joan Baez © Gabriel Earl Music, 1981.

"Garden Gathering" from The Talk of the Town, August 23, 1969. Reprinted by permission; © 1969 *The New Yorker Magazine, Inc.*

Daybreak by Joan Baez. Copyright © 1966, 1968 by Joan Baez. Reprinted by permission.

PICTURE ACKNOWLEDGMENTS

AP/Wide World Photos—pages 4, 49 (top right & bottom), 50 (top), 51 (top left & bottom right), 52 (3 photos), 53 (top left & right), 54 (3 photos), 98

UPI/Bettmann Newsphotos—pages 8, 49 (top left), 50 (bottom), 51 (top right & bottom left), 53 (bottom)

Photos courtesy of Joan Baez, Sr.—pages 47 (3 photos), 48 (3 photos)

Cover illustration by Len W. Meents

Library of Congress Cataloging-in-Publication Data

Heller, Jeffrey.
    Joan Baez : singer with a cause / by Jeffrey Heller.
        p.   cm. — (People of distinction)
    Includes bibliographical references and index.
    Summary: A biography of the singer whose songs motivated young people in the 1960s to take an interest in the world around them.
    ISBN 0-516-03271-2
    1. Baez, Joan—Juvenile literature. 2. Singers—United States—Biography—Juvenile literature. 3. Political activists—United States—Biography—Juvenile literature. [1. Baez, Joan. 2. Singers. 3. Political activists.] I. Title. II. Series.
ML3930.B205H4   1991
782.42162'13'0092—dc20
[B]   90-21046
                                                                  CIP
                                                                AC MN

Table of Contents

Chapter 1
Good Morning, Children of the Eighties   9

Chapter 2
Joan as a Symbol   17

Chapter 3
A Desperately Serious Star   27

Chapter 4
Turmoil in the United States   37

Chapter 5
Someone Had to Save the World   55

Chapter 6
Nonviolent Soldiers   67

Chapter 7
Timeless But Not Timely   79

Chapter 8
Bash On, Regardless   91

Appendix   99

Notes   100

Time Line   102

Index   105

Chapter 1

GOOD MORNING, CHILDREN OF THE EIGHTIES

In October 1984, a thirty-two-year-old rock-and-roll singer from Ireland named Bob Geldof watched a television program that made him physically ill, disgusted, and above all, angry. The program concerned the people of Ethiopia, a nation on the east coast of Africa.

A prolonged dry spell had ruined much of Ethiopia's farmland. Now a civil war within Ethiopia was preventing what little food could be grown there from reaching many people who needed it. Thousands of Ethiopian men, women, and children were starving.

Sitting comfortably in his living room, Bob Geldof saw the first television pictures to reach the outside world that showed Ethiopia's man-made disaster. The segment of the program that angered him the most showed a nurse choosing three hundred people to be fed, out of ten thousand who were all desperately hungry. "What separated those chosen to live from those condemned to die was a waist-high wall," said Geldof. "The people picked to be fed stood ashamed of their good fortune on one side of the wall, turning their backs in shame on the others. The ones left behind, in effect condemned to die, stood and watched with a beautiful dignity."[1]

Desperate to do something—anything—to help these starving people, Geldof decided to make a record to raise money for food. He was determined to send this food to Ethiopia somehow. By November 1984 he and a group of singers who called themselves "Band Aid" had assembled in a shabby recording studio to record a song called, "Do They Know It's Christmas?" Geldof and his friends—who included Sting, Phil Collins, and Bono from the group U2—hoped the group's record might earn $100,000. But how many people, they wondered, could be moved to care about starving people they had never met?

"Do They Know It's Christmas?" earned $100,000 within one hour of the record's release. Eventually it sold more records in Great Britain than any other record in history. Worldwide the song raised $11 million. Obviously a world full of people cared about others who didn't have enough to eat.

The money raised by Band Aid purchased 150 tons of high-energy crackers, along with 1,335 tons of powdered milk, 470 tons of sugar, and 1,000 tons of grain. Band Aid chartered three ships to transport the food and supplies to Africa, where professional relief agencies could begin moving the supplies into the heart of starving Ethiopia.

Geldof realized that sending these supplies to Ethiopia

was like dropping a single bead of water into a deep and empty well. What more could he do, not only to raise money but also to raise the consciousness of people around the world? By January 1985, he had an answer: organize a concert that would run sixteen hours long, one in Great Britain and one in the United States on the same day in July, featuring the world's most famous pop-music stars. People would buy tickets and, during the concert, they could pledge additional funds over the telephone.

At first, even Geldof wasn't sure he was serious. In July most rock stars are in the middle of tours. Even if they wanted to participate—a big "if"—they could never be assembled in one or two places at the same time. Most of his well-meaning friends told Geldof his idea of a "Live Aid" concert would never work.

But over the next several months Geldof badgered, pressured, and pursued every pop-music star he knew, and many he didn't know. Some groups said they would perform, then pulled out. Others waited to see who else would agree. By early summer, some of music's biggest names—like Eric Clapton, Mick Jagger, David Bowie, and the group Dire Straits—had said yes. Encouraged, Geldof took the final step and announced his dream publicly to the world, that on July 13, 1985, Live Aid would definitely take place.

In the final month before Live Aid, Bob Geldof and his friends from Band Aid secured Wembley Stadium outside

London and JFK Stadium in Philadelphia as the concert sites. Geldof also scrambled to obtain as much free talent and assistance as he could find. The musicians, of course, knew they would not be paid.

But others also caught the spirit. British Airways lent Band Aid the supersonic plane, *Concorde*, for the day, so that some stars could perform in both sites. Police were persuaded to provide their services free. Professional concert promoters volunteered to help organize the efforts of stage, sound, and lighting experts. Expensive video technology was provided at cost. Sixteen satellites were commandeered to beam Live Aid almost everywhere in the world. The developing countries of Africa would see the program free of charge; all other countries would pay for it.

When July 13 dawned clear and sunny over America and Britain, more than 1.5 billion people from Iceland to Ghana were ready to watch the show. That day, 85 percent of the world's television sets would be tuned to Live Aid.

By 8:00 A.M. that morning, Eastern Standard Time, ninety thousand music fans of all ages were packed into JFK Stadium in Philadelphia and cheering for the show to begin. Many of them wondered who the first act would be, and what exciting collection of musicians, lights, and special effects would begin this once-in-a-lifetime extravaganza.

The opening act had arrived at the stadium only one half hour earlier. She brought with her no backup musicians and no special equipment, only an acoustical guitar. Wearing a yellow parachute skirt, a cobalt blue blouse, and a thick belt with big silver circles, she looked very pretty—but hardly like a pop superstar. In truth, she wasn't.

At forty-five years of age, Joan Chandos Baez had short, dark hair that was already streaked with gray. But her olive-colored skin, a legacy from her Mexican father, was still smooth and unlined, and the gaze from her brown eyes was as clear and direct as ever. Backstage most of the musicians younger than forty greeted her warmly, but in eerily similar ways: "My mother has all your albums." "I was raised on your music."

These responses didn't surprise Joan. Her last truly popular record album, *Diamonds and Rust*, had appeared ten years before Live Aid. Her last hit single, "The Night They Drove Old Dixie Down," was fourteen years old. Most of her fellow performers that day were selling millions of records. In 1985, Joan Baez couldn't even find a company that wanted to record her.

Joan had been "shamelessly thrilled" at being chosen to open Live Aid. Because so many performers were scheduled to appear, she had only six minutes on stage. Just before 9:00 A.M., she was led up to the curtain separating her from ninety thousand spectators and a worldwide television audience. She went down on one knee, which made her feel safer and closer to the ground. Her heart pounded restlessly in her chest. Through the curtain she could make out thousands of bobbing heads and waving arms.

Then the curtain opened, and this lone woman walked onto the stage with her guitar. Upon hearing her name announced, many teenagers in the audience looked at each other and asked, "Who?" Then she leaned into the microphone and announced, "Good morning, Children of the Eighties. This is your Woodstock, and it's long overdue." An enormous roar went up from the crowd. Many were probably not sure why they were cheering, except that her words sounded reassuring.

The forty-something adults watching that day couldn't help but smile at her opening words. They knew that of all the musicians who would appear that day, Joan Baez was one of the few who also had appeared almost twenty years earlier at Woodstock, the first of the great pop music concerts.

"And it's nice to know the money out of your pockets will go to food to feed hungry children," she said next. "I can think of no more glorious way of starting our part of the day than by saying grace together, which means that we thank each of us, his and her own God, for the many blessings that we have in a world in which so many people have nothing. And when we say this grace, we also reach deep in our hearts and our souls and say that we will move a little from the comfort of our lives to understand their hurt, their pain, and their discomfort. And that will make their lives richer and it will make our lives real."[2]

Joan then said grace in a special way, by singing the spiritual "Amazing Grace." She had chosen it to appeal to the fans who had grown up with her music. She sang the opening verse *a cappella.*

> Amazing grace, how sweet the sound
> That saved a soul like me.
> I once was lost, but now I'm found.
> Was blind, but now I see.

Her voice was no longer the flawless, "achingly pure" soprano that music critics had loved when Joan Baez first caught the world's attention in 1960. But her voice was still a strong, clear voice that cut like a knife through the chatter of the ninety-thousand, restless audience. Bob Geldof had chosen his opening act well.

For those who didn't know her, hearing the voice of Joan Baez was a revelation. For those who did, it was a reminder of a time, only twenty years earlier, when her songs had helped mobilize young people to take an interest in the world around them for the first time.

Around the world, thousands of people watching Live Aid on television immediately recognized Joan Baez and welcomed her into their homes. Over nearly three decades she had sung from hundreds of concert stages in Europe, Africa, and South America. Perhaps more than her American audience, these people felt the hope and optimism that powered the distinctive voice and spirit of Joan Baez.

Her next and final song was "We Are the World" by Michael Jackson and Lionel Richie. As she began strumming her guitar, she said, "Sing this with me. This is the largest audience you'll ever have in your lives."[3] And everyone joined in.

Backstage after her performance, pop stars and their managers were talking into TV cameras about how terrific it felt to give their time and talents to help starving people. Joan wasn't interested in making such comments. She knew that a pop concert, even one that would eventually raise $70 million, could not end world hunger. She was prepared to sing out and speak out for the hungry and homeless people of the world long after Live Aid was a fond memory. After all, she'd been doing exactly that for almost thirty years.

For today, she had done her part. Now she wanted to gossip with her friends and flirt with all the attractive stars of music and television who had flocked to Philadelphia. She especially liked Don Johnson, the star of TV's "Miami Vice."

To a friend, she admitted that she hadn't really expected the audience to sing along with her. "The kids stopped singing 10 years ago," she said. Possibly they felt they hadn't inherited any cause worth singing about. Now with Live Aid, she said, they'd been given the chance to have a cause of their own.

Chapter 2

JOAN AS A SYMBOL

Since Joan Baez first became popular, many of her fans have tried to make her into a symbol of saintly goodness. Her enemies have tried to make her into a symbol of willful, self-centered disobedience to authority. Joan does believe she is a symbol, but of another kind entirely.

"I do think of myself as a symbol," she said recently, "of following through on your beliefs, using your talents to do so."[1]

Early in life, Joan learned from two special people, her parents, the importance of acting on her beliefs. Her father, Alberto Vinicio Baez, came to the United States at the age of two from Puebla, Mexico. He lived in Brooklyn, New York, where his father worked with poor and homeless people as a Methodist minister. Alberto intended to become a minister, too, but he changed his mind in favor of mathematics and finally physics.

Alberto was working his way through Drew University in Madison, New Jersey, when he met Joan Bridge. She had come to the United States from Edinburgh, Scotland, when she was a baby. Her father was an Episcopalian minister. Joan Bridge was attending a dance with another man when she first saw Alberto, a handsome man with thick, wavy, black hair and perfect white teeth. He was entertaining a group of girls by making airplane noises and dive-bombing motions with his hands. Alberto winked at Joan and she hurried off.

Another year went by before Alberto Baez took Joan Bridge out on a date in a model-T Ford that he had personally rebuilt into a race car. Alberto probably did not realize that he had found a woman as decisive and strong-willed as he.

Joan Bridge's father had married twice, and both wives were strange, violent women. Many years later, Joan Bridge told her daughters how she had declared her independence from her stepmother Meg. One day, Meg threw a pot of steaming boiled potatoes at thirteen-year-old Joan. Joan ducked the potatoes and continued what she was doing, washing the dishes. Meg came up and slapped Joan hard on the face. Then she raised her arms to beat Joan, but Joan caught her arms in midair and lowered them to Meg's sides, saying, "Don't you ever do that again."[2]

Meg backed off, and fumbling, handed Joan a pot so that she could go outside and pick berries. Joan said, "If you want berries, pick them yourself."[3] From that time on, Joan Bridge kept her coat hanging near the front door with two nickels in her pocket, one for bus fare and the other to call a friend.

Joan Bridge told her daughters that at some point in her childhood she had lived in a gypsy camp for a short time, eating potato crusts charcoaled over a fire. Even as a young girl, Joan Bridge would never let anyone push her around.

Within a year of their first date, Alberto Baez and Joan Bridge were married. Joan wanted girl children and she got them: Pauline Thalia was born in 1939, Joan Chandos in 1941, and Mimi Margharita in 1945.

Alberto pronounced his last name BISE, like MICE. But years later, when Joan became famous, *TIME* magazine explained to its readers that her last name was pronounced BUY-ezz. Joan was never able to correct this mistake, and that's how she is known today.

By the time Joan was four, her father had moved the family to Palo Alto, California, where he worked on his doctoral degree in mathematics at Stanford, California. Two years later, the Baez family was back in New York State, this time at Cornell University, where Alberto took a job as a research physicist.

Soon Alberto was invited to become head of Operations Research at Cornell. His work was top secret, but it evidently involved testing fighter jets, then a relatively new type of aircraft. He was offered a three-week cruise on an aircraft carrier and promised a huge salary.

Joan remembers her family's new-found prosperity. "We began to get new things like a vacuum cleaner, a refrigerator, a fancy coffeepot, and one day my father came home with a little Crosley car," she says. "We were so excited about it that we drove it all over the front lawn, around the trees and through the piles of leaves. He was driving, Mother was in the front seat, and we three kids were in the back. The neighbors knew we were odd to begin with, but this confirmed it."[4]

The Baez home had always been filled with music. At Sunday dinner, Alberto (whom Joan called "Popsy") loved to play recordings of music composed by Bach, Brahms, or Beethoven. Alberto would hum with the music while his three daughters pinched and swatted each other under the table.

Now Joan began taking piano lessons. After she had learned some of the basics, Joan remembers, "I searched [my piano book] for the shortest song, with the least number of sharps and flats, and taught myself, note for note, Beethoven's Sonata in G (opus 42)."[5]

Unfortunately, the family's prosperity would not last. Alberto knew that he probably could make an excellent living designing fighter planes, bombs, and other weapons. But he began to question whether this was the right thing for him to do. In California, the Baez family had been Presbyterians. Now Joan's mother suggested that the family change churches, hoping that her husband could find new spiritual guidance and direction. She chose the Quakers.

"Quaker Meeting—what a horror!" Joan remembers. "A room full of drab grown-ups who sat like ramrods with their eyes closed, or gazed blissfully at the ceiling."[6] Quaker meetings had no choir, no organ, no singing at all. The only sounds that broke the silence were the rumbles of tummies, the clearing of throats, and an occasional message from someone who was moved to stand up and speak. Even the twenty-minute sessions attended by the children seemed endless to Joan.

But in what Joan remembers as the silence of the first meetings, her father struggled with his conscience and made a decision. Rather than continuing to do defense work, he would become a professor.

Everyone except Joan's mother advised Alberto not to make the change. But he did. In Joan's words: "We would never have all the fine and useless things little girls want when they are growing up. Instead we would have a father with a clear conscience. Decency would be his legacy to us."[7]

Soon the Baez family was moving again, first to California and then, of all places, to the Middle Eastern country of Iraq. In 1951, Alberto took a job with UNESCO (the United Nations Educational, Scientific and Cultural Organization) to teach and build a physics lab at the University of Baghdad. Joan remembers living in this mysterious city and moving her bed on warm nights to the roof of the family home. There she would sleep under the stars and dream that the king of Iraq, then only twelve, would come prancing down her street on a white horse, pick the ten-year-old girl with olive skin out of a crowd, and tell Joan she was beautiful.

It was in Iraq that Joan's passion for social justice was born. She had always known, somehow, that children in other parts of the world went to bed hungry at night. But during her year in Iraq she often saw "animals beaten to death, people rooting for food in our family garbage pails, and legless children dragging themselves along the streets on cardboard . . . begging for money."[8] Far from being repelled or disgusted, Joan felt great sympathy for these wretched people.

Within a year the Baez family had returned to Redlands, California, where Joan faced a new problem: her ethnic background. Junior high school was filled with the children of Mexican immigrants and illegal aliens who picked fruit in local fields. The boys were *pachucos*, tough guys with gorgeous, slick-backed hair and pegged pants worn low on the hip. The girls wore tight skirts, nylons, violet lipstick, and masses of frizzed-up hair. At school these kids banded together, speaking Spanish.

"By contrast, I was Joanie Boney," Joan remembers. "An awkward stringbean . . . my hair a bunch of black straw whacked off just below my ears . . . my blouse too big, my shoes scuffed, my lunch bag many times used . . . and no lipstick."[9]

22

Now here she was, with a Mexican name, skin, and hair. The Anglos couldn't accept Joan because of all three, and the Mexicans couldn't accept her because she didn't speak Spanish.

To make matters worse, Americans were now caught up in the antiCommunist panic of the mid-1950s, and most kids echoed their parents' belief in bombing the "Commies" before they bombed America. In contrast, Joan's armament-hating father would regularly bring friends home for political discussions, which Joan couldn't help overhearing. So Joan began to speak up politely in class about the silliness of seeking peace by building costly weapons systems. As a result, many of her classmates and their parents pegged Joan as the worst kind of troublemaker, a political one. Some parents even warned their children not to talk to her.

It was Joan's sense of isolation, of being different, that led her to develop her voice. She tried out for the girl's glee club at school, and amazingly, this future pop music star was turned down. But she didn't give up. She began singing in the shower, trying to stay on one note and force her voice up and down slowly. She thought this would make her voice sound more dramatic and "mature," but it didn't work.

However by bobbling one finger up and down on her Adam's apple, she could create the vocal effect she wanted. And for a few seconds, she could sound "mature" without using a finger on her throat. This is how Joan decided to begin training her voice. By summer's end, she had a "shaky but honest vibrato."[10] She was developing her own vocal style.

At the same time, Joan began taking lessons on the ukulele, a small guitar from Hawaii. She would listen to popular songs on a tiny, gray radio at her bedside, memorize the tunes by ear and scribble down the words. Then she would find the right key to sing each song. She was learning how to make other people's songs her own.

Before long, Joan was taking her ukulele to school and singing pop songs to the kids in the courtyard at lunchtime. She even did Elvis Presley imitations. Within a week this gawky outsider became something of a clown. But she loved the attention. "I live on glory,"[11] she confided to her diary as a fourteen year old.

A few friends suggested that she sing in a school talent show. Unlike many future pop stars, Joan was not an overnight sensation. She didn't win the prize. But she learned two important lessons at Redlands High School: first, that her legs trembled terribly when she performed (and no matter how famous and popular she became later, an almost overwhelming fear of performing has never left her). Second, Joan learned she had a talent for bluffing. "If you look and act enough as if you know what your [sic] doing," she wrote in her diary, "it deceives about 99/100% of the people watching."[12]

Joan continued singing and performing during her years at Palo Alto High School after her father moved the family back to Palo Alto and Stanford in time for her eleventh-grade year. She sang at college proms and student conferences and for her parents and their friends at home. Once she even sang at a high school so far out of town that it paid for her air transportation. Although she was now dating, most of her romantic activity took place while she performed. "I flirted furiously from behind my guitar, sometimes staring into the eyes of one unsuspecting boy for an entire song," she remembers. "I flirted and sang, and developed a reputation for both."[13]

She also developed a reputation for speaking her mind, politely but firmly. Once she and her high school classmates were told that an air-raid drill would be held the next day. When three bells sounded, the students were to go home. That night, Joan hunted through her father's books. She discovered that a guided missile traveled so quickly that if the Russians attacked, students in America would never have time to calmly leave their seats and find their way home once the missile had been spotted. Her high school's air-raid drill was useless.

The next day, as the three bells sounded, Joan remained seated in her French class. The teacher, whom she liked, waved her to the door, and with a pounding heart, she explained that she was protesting the stupidity of the air-raid drill. The teacher finally left, muttering French curses under his breath. Joan was alone in her school.

The day after the air-raid drill, Joan was on the front page of the local newspaper. Readers wrote to the editor about Communists infiltrating the high school. But both of Joan's parents seemed pleased with her protest. Perhaps, they felt, she was serious about something other than boys.

Joan's parents were not entirely correct. At a student conference run by the Quakers, Joan remembers falling in love with ten or twelve boys at once. But she doesn't remember their names, only the name of the conference's main speaker, a twenty-seven-year-old black preacher from Alabama named Martin Luther King, Jr.

King "talked . . . about fighting with the weapons of love, saying that when someone does evil to us, we can hate the evil deed but not the doer of the deed," she recalls. "When he finished his speech, I was on my feet, cheering and crying."[14] For the first time, someone had given a shape and a name to Joan's passionately held set of beliefs. King called it "nonviolence."

This revelation did not change Joan's essential view of herself. "I love to be the center of attention, and pardon the conceit, I usually am," she once wrote in her diary. "I spend a good deal of my time making wise cracks, singing, dancing, acting, and . . . making a nuisance of myself. I am not a saint. I am a noise."[15]

Chapter 3

A DESPERATELY SERIOUS STAR

In the summer of 1958, the Baez family moved to Boston, where Alberto took a job at Massachusetts Institute of Technology. Driving across the country with her mother and sisters, Joan first heard a song on the radio that would change her life—and the course of American pop music—forever.

Hang down your head, Tom Dooley,

Hang down your head and cry,

Hang down your head, Tom Dooley,

Poor boy, you're bound to die.

Compared to most pop music of the late 1950s, "Tom Dooley" was terribly sad. A man has stabbed his lady love to death, and now he is going to hang for his crime. Three young men who called themselves The Kingston Trio sang the song without an orchestra or rock band, using only acoustical guitars to back up their voices.

"Tom Dooley" wasn't pop music and it certainly wasn't the pure folk music of American mountain people. But somehow this mixture of folk and pop music reached young city dwellers who were tiring of 1950s-style rock and roll. The recording sold 2.6 million copies. Something new was happening.

Not long after the Baez family settled into a house outside Boston, the ever-curious Alberto took his daughter Joan to examine a new phenomenon sprouting up in Harvard Square: the "coffeehouse." But where Alberto approvingly saw young people reading, holding intellectual discussions, and playing chess over their coffee, Joan heard young performers playing and singing. They sang Kingston Trio songs, along with folk ballads that originally came from England and Scotland. Joan had enrolled at Boston University's School of Drama and hated every minute of it. Now, she remembers, "I wanted to move into Harvard Square and fall in love with every guitar player and singer I met."[1]

New girlfriends taught Joan songs such as "Fair and Tender Maidens" and "All My Trials." Like "Tom Dooley," these songs focused so intensely on death, misery, and heartbreak that Joan would often weep while trying to learn them on the classical guitar she had just purchased. At seventeen, Joan began singing duets with a girlfriend at local coffeehouses. She couldn't wait until her short hair grew out into waist-length tresses, so she could look like the tragic, lovesick maidens in her songs.

One day as she sat on the banks of the Charles River practicing her guitar, a young Harvard student rowed over to her in a small boat. Michael New, a nineteen-year-old English boy raised in Trinidad, West Indies, said a shy hello and soon rowed off. But it was enough. He had blue eyes, a finely chiseled nose, and golden tousled hair. Joan was entranced.

Through friends she discovered that Michael spoke French as well as English, had no girlfriend, and hated the United States. He sounded perfect. What is more, they told her, Michael seemed just as interested in her. Joan searched for Michael in the stores and student hangouts around Harvard Square.

By the winter of 1958, Joan and Michael had found each other and were together every possible moment.

"When I first saw snowflakes on Michael's hair, they looked so beautiful that I wanted to be one of them and melt down through to the roots and then under his skin and just live there, because that was where I belonged,"[2] she wrote many years later.

Now Joan dropped completely out of Boston University, where she was flunking all her courses. She was offered a job singing on two "folk nights" a week at Club Mt. Auburn 47 in Harvard Square. For each performance she received $10. Her first audience amounted to eight people, including her mother and father, her sister Mimi, and two friends. "It was a ridiculous situation, friends and family all trying to look like an audience, trying not to peer hopefully over at the door every time they heard footsteps,"[3] Joan says. But when she returned the following Tuesday, the tiny club was half filled. Slowly she was building an audience.

Michael's dream was to build something else: a boat for sailing away to an island where he and Joan could live alone, together, forever. To Joan that sounded just fine. "Michael was my God, and I didn't question him because I didn't want to lose him,"[4] she said years later.

But if she tended to bow to Michael's opinions behind closed doors, on stage Joan was turning into a tyrant. As her repertoire of songs expanded, her rigidity remained the same. Each new song was as desperately serious as the last. After enough listeners began to giggle at Joan's unrelenting parade of musical misery, she added some humorous numbers to her show. It was the first of many concessions to her audience. But at this point, Joan says, "I was very *stuffy* about my music."[5]

What's more, she remembers, "If some innocent student wandered into the coffee house thinking it was like all the others, namely a place to relax and read, he was mistaken. I'd stop in the middle of a song and tell him that if he wanted to study he could use the library."[6]

By day, Joan held other jobs, such as teaching people how to ride Vespa motor scooters and taking them to get their licenses. But Joan's career as a singer was starting to move faster. With two other young singers, Joan sang on a home-made record album and prepared for her first concert. It was advertised on posters around Harvard Square. Confronted with "Joan Baez" in bright letters, she seriously considered changing her first name to Rachel or Mariah, and possibly her last name as well. But at the last minute she decided against it, fearing that people might think she was ashamed of her Mexican background.

Joan also attracted admiring boys, which quickly made Michael very jealous. Joan was enjoying her local fame and all the attention she received from male fans. She really didn't want to sail away to an island. She and Michael started fighting. Joan also began seeing a psychiatrist to help her deal with the many tensions in her life.

That summer, while Michael was visiting his parents in Trinidad, a young music promoter named Albert Grossman approached Joan and asked her to sing in his club. The Gate of Horn, in Chicago, was one of the country's best-known clubs for folk performers. Grossman offered Joan $200 a week for two weeks' work, but Joan was frightened. She was only eighteen.

After talking with her parents, Joan decided to go to Chicago. "I was frightened of flying alone, of staying alone, of a club where people drank and might not listen, of everything, and that's why I went,"[7] she says today.

For Joan, the Gate of Horn was the right place at the right time. In 1959, the explosion of folk-oriented coffeehouses, which began in Boston, was spreading throughout the United States. New groups such as the Limelighters, the Chad Mitchell Trio, and Peter, Paul and Mary would soon be competing with The Kingston Trio for America's attention.

Best of all, no threat to the new folk music was in sight. Across the Atlantic Ocean, in Liverpool, England, a fresh-faced boy named Paul McCartney was only sixteen. And in 1959, Paul was still planning to attend teacher training college, although a new friend, John Lennon, was pressing Paul to take more seriously the rock-and-roll music they were performing in their band, the Quarry Men. Not for another five years would this band, renamed the Beatles, score their first hit record in America and push folk music off center stage.

Joan's two weeks at the Gate of Horn left her baffled, flattered, and terrified. She also learned, from more experienced performers such as Bob Gibson, that a folk performer could laugh and joke with an audience and sing silly songs as well as serious ones. If she wanted to, she could entertain people. When she wasn't performing, she spent her time practicing new songs and reading letters from Michael about how he doubted her loyalty to him every minute of the day. Since meeting him, Joan had not dated any other men. But in a way, Michael was right.

That August, Bob Gibson invited Joan to appear as his guest at the first Folk Festival in Newport, Rhode Island. On the festival's second night, Bob was happily entertaining thirteen thousand folk music fans who sat in an open field, not bothered by a misty rain. Just offstage, Joan stood clutching her guitar with sweaty hands. She wore a bright orange, silk-lined Mexican blouse. On her feet were thong gladiator sandals that laced up to just below her knees.

Then Joan heard Bob announce that he had a guest. "In that moment there was only the speeding of my heart; all movement was a silent film, and all sound was surface noise," she recalls. "There were nods of encouragement and thumbs up all around. It is my style when I am let out of the chute to walk swiftly and steadily, and I did so up the soggy stairs to my doom or glory."[8]

To Joan, the audience at Newport looked like the biggest crowd ever assembled in the history of the world. She sang two songs with Bob, and after each one people applauded wildly. Both songs were religious and Joan recollects she looked and sounded "like purity itself in long tresses, no makeup, and Bible sandals."[9] The next day, local news accounts labeled her "the Madonna" and "the Virgin Mary"—two descriptions that Joan happily accepted at the time, but that haunted and frustrated her for years.

With the Newport concert Joan felt she had made an important step forward. "In the book of my destiny the first page had been turned, and . . . this book could no longer be exchanged for any other."[10]

Back in Boston she continued performing at the Club 47. She also met two brothers from New York, Maynard and Seymour Solomon. The Solomons ran a record company called Vanguard, which recorded classical music. The Solomons said they wanted to make a "quality record" of Joan's songs. Albert Grossman wanted her to sign with Columbia Records. But Joan felt more at home with the Solomon brothers' love of classical music and their casual but intellectual manner. She talked with her parents and her friends. Then she made her own decision. She signed a contract with Vanguard.

Michael returned from Trinidad, Joan began working as a housemother at Perkins Institute for the Blind, and her music making continued. That winter, Perkins fired Joan for going barefoot and looking too much like a hippie (though that word had not yet been coined). Joan also continued to love, and fight with, Michael.

One day Joan was driving through Harvard Square and saw Michael in front of a bookstore. He was leaning forward to kiss a woman on the lips. Joan parked down the street and waited long enough to see Michael race back to his dormitory for their meeting. She recounts that "He yawned and put his book down when I walked in, and I watched him lie for the first time."[11]

In the summer of 1960 Michael once again returned home. And Joan went to New York City to make her first album for Vanguard. It all seemed very casual to Joan. The Solomons' recording studio was a ballroom in a dingy hotel. On Wednesdays residents and guests used the room for bingo.

Joan stood on a dirty rug in her bare feet and sang into three microphones. A fourth mike was added when Joan decided, after much thought, that having a backup guitar player would not compromise the integrity of her music. For a few hours she would sing, then everyone would break for roast beef sandwiches. Some songs were covered in one attempt or "take." "As long as a dog didn't run through the room or something, you had it,"[12] Joan remembers. In three days Joan recorded nineteen songs, thirteen of which made up her first solo album.

Recording was easy compared to the prospect of living on her own. But shortly after she returned to Boston, her parents informed Joan that they were moving back to California. For the first time, Alberto and Joan, two of her most loyal fans, would not be there to support her. She and a girlfriend moved in together, and Michael soon joined them.

But relations with Michael were growing more and more tense. One night in the middle of a routine argument, Joan grabbed a lamp and threw it across the room, hitting Michael squarely in the head. Moments later she smashed a wine bottle against the wall. She was heading for the plates in the kitchen when Michael grabbed her arms at the elbows. Without thinking, she grabbed his hair and pulled, kicking furiously at his ankles. Grabbing and hissing at each other, they both quickly collapsed in tears.

Michael left soon afterward, but he was back. And with

the resilience (or perhaps the stubbornness) of young lovers everywhere, they decided to make a new start. They discussed moving to California. After Joan gave a series of college concerts in the fall of 1960, she and Michael packed their belongings into a new Corvair and headed west.

When they arrived in California, a surprise awaited them. Joan's album, so casually and easily recorded over the summer, was released at Christmas. As Joan watched in amazement, the album called *Joan Baez* climbed to the number-three position among the top one hundred best-selling albums in the United States.

Chapter 4

TURMOIL IN THE UNITED STATES

In May 1961, a group of college-age young people, black and white, decided to challenge state laws in the South that forced black people to sit in the back of public buses. The students organized a series of "Freedom Rides" through the South to promote their cause.

When the Freedom Riders arrived at a Greyhound bus terminal in Montgomery, Alabama, they were met by a self-appointed welcoming committee. Angry Alabamians, with weapons such as baseball bats and metal pipes, screamed and yelled at the Freedom Riders.

Knowing the dangers they faced, the Freedom Riders had asked for protection from local police but when they arrived in their bus, no police officers were around. Students who left the bus were attacked by the crowd. Some were thrown over a fence to a parking lot below.

By the time the police arrived, the mob had injured twenty Freedom Riders. Ambulances that were called failed to arrive. President John F. Kennedy had to send hundreds of U.S. marshals to restore order. Alabama Governor John Patterson blamed the Freedom Riders for the riot. He felt they were the ones who caused the trouble.

Joan Baez's first successful record album arrived at a time of great racial turmoil and upheaval in the United States. Only four years earlier, in 1957, the United States Supreme Court had sparked what came to be called the civil rights movement. The court had declared that forcing blacks into supposedly "separate but equal" public schools, just to keep them away from whites, was against the law.

By 1960 young people of both races were demonstrating in the streets against the fact that blacks often were not allowed to use the same restaurants that white people could enjoy, nor the same hotels, parks, playgrounds, beaches, libraries, and movie theaters. Many demonstrations that began peacefully ended in fistfights with people who were just as fiercely committed to keeping things as they were. Black people's churches, schools, and homes were bombed and burned. Blacks and whites marching to promote equal rights for everyone were beaten, stabbed, and shot.

The year Freedom Riders began, Joan Baez toured the South for the first time. Like most Americans, she wasn't very aware of the civil rights movement at the time. But she soon realized that no black people ever came to her concerts. Few of them knew who she was. But even if they did, and they wanted to hear her sing, in many Southern towns black people weren't allowed to sit with white people at the same concert. The next time she came to the South, Joan decided, she would not let this happen.

After her tour, Joan returned to her new home in Carmel, California—and to Michael. "We were inseparable and couldn't imagine each other with anyone else,"[1] she remembers. As her first record continued to sell and she became better known, Joan began to speak out more at her concerts. She talked about the concept of nonviolence formulated by Martin Luther King, Jr. However, Michael disapproved of her interest in changing the world and because she didn't want to lose him, she held herself back from openly participating in civil rights demonstrations.

Still success began to change her life. Joan gave only twenty concerts in 1961, but she earned enough money to make some startling purchases. She and Michael now rented a small cabin in Big Sur for only $35 a month. But one day, while walking to a hardware store to buy a flashlight, they passed a car showroom and ended up buying a silver Jaguar XLE for $6,000. To save money at home, Joan bought condensed milk. Yet she casually bought silk blouses and even cars for her friends.

That same year, she and Michael visited a folk club in New York City. There, Joan met the man who would replace Michael as the next great influence on her life. To Joan he resembled an urban hillbilly. He wore a leather jacket two sizes too small, and he bounced from foot to foot as he played his guitar and spat out the words to songs Joan found original and refreshing.

When his set was over, he was ushered to Joan and Michael's table. He had stringy, curly hair and a soft, sensuous mouth. "He was absurd, new, and grubby beyond words,"[2] Joan remembers. Naturally Michael didn't like him, but Joan remembers wishing that Michael would disappear so she could get to know this strange young man. His name was Bob Dylan.

"There was no question that this boy was exceptional and that he touched people," she recalls, "but he had only just begun to touch me."[3]

Joan made her second concert tour of the South in 1962. She insisted in her contract that she would not sing unless blacks were admitted to the concert halls. She also decided to sing at four black colleges.

Her appearance at Miles College in Birmingham, Alabama, was memorable for several reasons. The same day she was scheduled to sing, Martin Luther King, Jr. had organized a massive demonstration downtown. Joan arrived a few days early to meet with King. They stayed with their supporters and traveling companions in the only hotel in Birmingham that accepted both blacks and whites. At that time blacks had to search before finding a hotel that would admit them.

On Sunday morning, Joan was invited to sing at a local Baptist church that she and King attended. She remembers singing in a voice "very different from the pure white one which is on all my records. I sang with the soul I was adopting right there in that room and heads began to nod in approval, and wrinkled old faces smiled in confusion and pleasure."[4]

The day of her concert, blacks and whites marched through downtown Birmingham. They were met with fire hoses, tear gas, attack dogs, and arrests. Joan was furious that she couldn't be with them but she had to honor her commitment at Miles College. Before the show, as she was talking with her hosts on the college lawn, white people began to arrive in small groups. They walked into the main building where Joan would sing. Joan's hosts said they were the first white people ever to set foot on the campus.

During the concert, everyone seemed very aware of the arrests and violence taking place downtown. When Joan ended her concert by singing "We Shall Overcome," the entire audience rose as one and held hands, swaying back and forth as they joined in singing. Many of them were crying.

Back home, many pressures on Joan were intensifying. The more independent and assertive she became, the more Michael tried to tighten his hold on her. She began doubling up on her sessions with the psychiatrist.

The national media increased the pressure by depicting Joan as a practically perfect heroine of the young people's movement, or counterculture.

By November the major magazines and newspapers were singing a different tune. *HORIZON* magazine commented that instead of searching for her songs as folk musicologists do, by carrying tape recorders through small rural villages, Joan simply selected from what she heard or from the songs people sent her.

TIME magazine described her unique appeal: ". . . her most typical selections are so mournful and quietly desperate that her early records would not be out of place at a funeral."[5] *TIME* also seemed puzzled at her lack of interest in folk history. "I don't care very much about where a song came from or why or even what it says," Joan innocently told a *TIME* interviewer. "All I care about is how it sounds and the feeling in it."[6]

But clearly, declared *TIME*, Joan was someone special. "In performance she comes on, walks straight to the microphone, and begins to sing. No patter. No show business. . . . The purity of her voice suggests purity of approach. . . . It is haunted and plaintive, a mother's voice, and it has in it distant reminders of black women wailing in the night, of detached madrigal singers performing calmly at court, and of saddened gypsies trying to charm death into leaving their Spanish caves."[7]

All of this praise was a genuine shock to Joan, and she regrets today that she so readily accepted the pristine image painted of her by the media. "Up until then . . . the only image I had of myself was of a dumb Mexican. I'd come from a place where Mexicans were called dumb peach-pickers. So I already had a big identity problem . . . and all of a sudden somebody said, 'Bingo, you're the Madonna with the achingly pure soprano.' Well, who isn't gonna opt for that, if those are your choices?"[8]

Ironically she made the cover of *TIME* in November, but the portrait of this supposedly wonderful person made Joan look deathly ill. And that's because she was. Feverish and racked with stomach spasms while the portrait was being painted, Joan was soon admitted to the hospital, malnourished and dehydrated. She weighed only 102 pounds. When Michael came to visit her against doctor's orders, Joan truly wished he was dead.

Joan's second record album was now released. It sold even better than the first one. But Joan was too upset and emotionally strained to enjoy her success.

A few weeks later, Joan journeyed to New York to sing on a television show. One night she wrote a letter to Michael. She told him about his lovely eyes and how wonderful the first three months of their relationship had been. And she told him good-bye. The last time she saw him he appeared at her dressing room a few weeks later just before a concert. He was apologetic and full of promises but Joan eventually succeeding in saying good-bye. On that sad note, after four years together, they parted company for good.

Joan's third album appeared in 1963. Her audiences had grown from three thousand people at town halls to as many as twenty thousand people at the Hollywood Bowl. Her hair, now very long and straight, produced an effect that was "biblical but gloomy,"[9] says Joan today. At this point in her career, she realized that she could do something more with her life than just sing and make lots of money.

One of her first steps into the future involved Bob Dylan, who was still largely unknown. In August she asked him to sing at her concerts. People who hadn't heard of him often booed him. Joan would respond by shaking her fingers at the offenders like a schoolmarm. She advised them to listen to the songs Bob Dylan wrote because he was a genius.

Young readers today might have a difficult time understanding the appeal of Bob Dylan. He was sloppy and dirty looking, not handsome or sexy in any conventional way. Quite unlike Joan, he had a strained and whiny voice that garbled even the prettiest melodies he wrote. And where Joan tried to be gracious with people who disagreed with her, Dylan tended to be condescending and downright rude even with people who claimed to adore him.

But in his own odd way, Bob reached people as intensely as Joan did. In the late 1980s, Bruce Springsteen expressed it simply by saying, "The way that Elvis freed your body, Bob freed your mind."[10]

Perhaps Bob's appeal reveals itself most clearly through

Joan's eyes. "His humor was dry, private and splendid. . . .
He was rarely tender, and seldom reached out to anticipate
another's needs . . . He was touching and infinitely fragile . . .
He seemed to function from the center of his own thoughts
and images, and like a madman he was swallowed up by
them. . . ."[11]

"Everyone wanted to be the one to get under his skin, to
say the clever thing which would make him laugh . . . He
held us all at a distance except for rare moments, which we
all sought."[12]

For a very short time that Joan doesn't specify, she and
Bob lived together in a crummy, New York City hotel. They
would sing and laugh, talk, ride motorcycles, and go to
movies. "I was . . . sister mystic and fellow outlaw, queen to
his jack, and a twin underground star," she remembers. "I
was falling in love."[13] But Dylan's popularity was growing to
match her own, and when that happened, their relationship
would never again be simple and carefree.

What Joan loved most of all about Bob Dylan was his
music. Songs like "Blowin' in the Wind" and "The Times
They Are A-Changin'" seemed to make the human struggle
for justice very real and personal to Joan. These and other
songs began to propel her out of the world of old English and
Scottish ballads and into the music scene of the 1960s.

In August of 1963, Martin Luther King, Jr. gave his
famous "I Have a Dream" speech to more than 350,000 peo-

ple gathered before the Lincoln Memorial in Washington, D.C. Joan was invited to sing and she led the huge crowd in "We Shall Overcome." President Kennedy was so moved by King's speech that he asked Congress for an all-embracing civil rights law that would forbid anyone from denying blacks the use of all public facilities, including hotels, motels, and restaurants.

But three months later John F. Kennedy was dead, shot by a sniper's bullet in Dallas, Texas. Joan had been asked to sing at a gala for Kennedy, which now would be held for the nation's new president. Joan had her doubts about singing for Lyndon Johnson, the new president. But she decided that canceling her appearance was too rigid and would offend people unnecessarily.

Above: Alberto Vinicio and Joan Bridge Baez
Below: Joan at the age of three

Above: Joan, when she was about ten years old, and Joan with her sisters Pauline (left) and Mimi (right) Below: One of the family's favorite photographs, taken in 1953, shows (left to right) Pauline, Joan, Sr., Mimi, and Joan, Jr.

Above: In 1965, Joan was in London with Bob Dylan. The year before, she could still smile although the Internal Revenue Service had filed a $50,000 lien against her for nonpayment of taxes. Below: Joan entertains a group of students demonstrating in a free-speech movement at the University of California, Berkeley.

In the midst of the civil rights desegregation movement, Joan carries the books of a black child as she walks her to school in Grenada, Mississippi (right) on September 19, 1966. The next day, Joan accompanies a group, led by Reverend Martin Luther King, Jr., escorting black children to their newly integrated school (below).

Left: In 1968 Joan and David Harris were wed and their son, Gabriel Earl (below), was born in 1969.

Left: David Harris speaks to students at San Francisco State College about resisting the draft. Above: Joan is greeted by her son, Gabe, after she returns from her trip to Hanoi, North Vietnam, in 1973.

Joan and Bob Dylan sing in a
performance in Madison
Square Garden in New York
(above) in 1975 and Joan
performs in a Kent State
concert (above right) in 1977.
In 1979, Joan meets with her
father, "Popsy," outside the
National Press Club (right) in
Washington, D.C., where
Joan was scheduled to speak
about her trip to Cambodia.

Joan and Bob Dylan sing at "Peace Sunday" (above left) in Pasadena in 1982. Earlier Joan had visited Southeast Asia. In Cambodia (above right), Joan holds a child in a refugee camp and in Hong Kong (below), she entertains Vietnamese refugee children.

Joan likes performing at the Newport Folk Festival in Newport, Rhode Island. In 1985 (above left) she sings with Arlo Guthrie and in 1990 (above right) Joan sings on opening day. Backstage in 1984 (below) Joan enjoys a laugh with Judy Collins and Joan's sister Mimi Farina.

Chapter 5

SOMEONE HAD TO SAVE THE WORLD

On November 20, 1963, President John F. Kennedy told White House aide Michael Forrestal that he wanted him to study all the options the United States had in Vietnam, including withdrawing our troops.

Kennedy had inherited a major problem from the previous president. Once a colony of France, Vietnam had won its freedom after an eight-year war that ended in a truce in 1954. Free, country-wide elections were scheduled to be held one year later. However, high officials in the United States government decided that free elections would almost certainly bring to power the Communists who had led Vietnam's eight-year war against France.

Rather than take this risk, the United States acted to transform the temporary southern zone of Vietnam into a separate and permanent nation. A politician named Ngo Dihn Diem was installed as the head of this new nation, called South Vietnam, and the United States kept him well supplied with money and supplies.

By the time Kennedy took office in 1960, Diem's government was widely hated by many South Vietnamese. A secret meeting of Diem's enemies resulted in the formation of armed guerrilla units known as Viet Cong. Kennedy then increased United States aid to Diem. He also increased the number of American soldiers (called "advisers") in Vietnam from ten thousand to twenty thousand. They had orders to shoot back if fired upon.

By 1963 South Vietnam's civil war was going badly. Diem's United States-supported army could not hold more than one-third of the country against the Viet Cong. Kennedy seriously considered withdrawing all United States troops after he was reelected in 1964. At that point, he might have decided to continue fighting. No one will ever know. Two days after making his request to Forrestal, Kennedy was dead.

In 1964 Joan Baez released her fourth album, a live concert recording. And once more, young Americans—and Joan—were in turmoil.

At first President Lyndon Johnson vowed not to get American troops involved in Vietnam. But his determination not to lose this war led him to increase steadily the number of troops he sent there. That summer, the *New York Times* revealed that Johnson had secretly promised South Vietnamese leaders that the United States would bomb the other half of this divided country, called North Vietnam, as soon as the fall 1964 elections were over.

All over America, many young people felt Johnson's actions were immoral and unfair. Why is America propping up a government that most South Vietnamese don't seem to want? Why should we interfere at all? Many people felt we should let the people in North and South Vietnam decide their own future.

At this point Joan made a dangerous decision. She figured that defense costs amounted to 60 percent of the national budget. So she sent the federal Internal Revenue Service (IRS) a letter stating that she refused to pay 60 percent of her federal income taxes. "We plan and build weapons that can take thousands of lives in a second, millions of lives in a day, billions in a week," her letter stated. "No one has the right to do that."[1] At the same time, Joan released this letter to the press.

In no time, the IRS claimed her house, car, and land. Joan said she didn't care. Sometimes an IRS official would appear at her concerts and take cash from the register before it even reached Joan. She soon realized the government would obtain all of its money from her, plus fines. But she still refused to just give her money to the government. It would have to waste its own time and resources to obtain her money.

Joan continued refusing to pay her income taxes for ten years. She also began appearing on television talk shows to speak with audience members about the United States involvement in Vietnam.

Now alerted to the presence of a troublemaker, government agencies began keeping a file of Joan's movements, statements, and activities. Within another five years more than fifteen hundred agents of the U.S. army were keeping files on thousands of citizens with views similar to Joan's, including Senator Adlai Stevenson II, child authority Dr. Benjamin Spock, and civil rights leader Julian Bond. Joan probably took this spying for granted. She didn't realize that government agents also would find more aggressive ways to undermine her efforts.

Life in 1964 was not entirely grim for Joan. Bob Dylan invited her to share a house with him for a month in Woodstock, New York. They enjoyed riding his 350 Triumph motorcycle through the woods. "He is beautiful to me," Joan wrote her parents. "And he's just a joy to be with. We understand each other's need for freedom and there are no chains, just good feelings and giggles and a lot of love."[2]

After a month in Woodstock, Joan returned to California. By early 1965 she and Bob were together again for a short concert tour. Each sang for forty minutes, then they sang together to close the show. In Denver Joan met the Beatles on one of their first American tours.

However differences and tensions soon surfaced between Bob and Joan. One year earlier, Bob had commented that Joan was "still singin' about Mary Hamilton [an old English ballad]. I mean where's that at? She's walked around on picket lines, she's got all kinds of feeling, so why ain't she steppin' out?"[3] In fact, she was and Bob was not. Bob never went on a march, and he pointedly left the protesting to others. What he wanted Joan to do, he was obviously not willing to do himself.

Their differences came to a head when Bob toured England for the first time in the spring of 1965. He invited Joan to join him, and she assumed he also would ask her to sing with him on stage. He would be returning the favor Joan had done him two years earlier. But he didn't. The documentary film *Don't Look Back*, still available in many video stores, wonderfully captures the way young English fans were bowled over by Dylan and the offbeat intensity that had originally captivated Joan. The film also shows Dylan, in his interviews and encounters with fans, to be completely absorbed in himself. He had grabbed the spotlight and didn't want to share it with anyone. Significantly, Joan appears in the film for only a few moments.

"For the first time in my short but monumentally successful career someone had stolen all my thunder from under my nose,"[4] Joan remembers. Joan was so upset at being completely ignored that one night she ran in tears to a mutual friend.

"But Bob *asked* me to come. He *asked* me," she cried.

"I know," said the friend. "But he don't know what's happening anymore, can't you see? He's just out there spinnin' and he wants to do it by himself."[5]

Joan said later that she should have shown enough sense to pack her bags immediately and go home. But when the tour ended she was still there, without Bob having once asked her to join him on stage. Joan eventually learned to accept the fact that this gifted man had flaws like any other human being. In the coming years, they would perform together many times. But Joan never again felt about him the way she did at age twenty-four.

Back in the United States, President Johnson was now convinced that the South Vietnamese army could never win the war on the land. So he committed 100,000 American soldiers to the battle, making the United States a full-fledged participant.

This action outraged many young Americans. At this time eighteen-year-olds could not vote, but they could be drafted into the armed forces. Many wondered why they were considered old enough to die for their country, but not old enough to vote. Like the Vietnam conflict itself, the intensity of student protests escalated. Many young men refused to be drafted. Others demonstrated to abolish the draft system and get the United States out of Vietnam.

Realizing the dilemmas that many young people now faced, Joan in 1965 wrote her parents a somber letter. "I must be ready not to die for something, but to live for it, which is really much harder," she wrote. "I have a choice of things to do with my life. I think it is time to charge in head first. I want to start a peace movement." She signed the letter, "Your egomaniacal daughter."[6]

The fact that Joan took herself so seriously and her certainty that she could change the world may seem innocent or foolish to today's young people. Even Joan said, years later, with a little sarcasm "Someone had to save the world. And, obviously, I felt I was the one for the job."[7] In the 1960s, many young people felt as Joan did. But few were as willing as Joan to back their words with action.

With some friends and her own money, Joan purchased a small house in Carmel Valley and opened the Institute for the Study of Nonviolence. In seminars and informal discussions, Joan and the many young people who attended the institute considered the use of nonviolence in both personal and international relationships. "The more I read and talked and argued and discussed, the more devoted I became to the concept,"[8] she says.

Joan realized that practicing nonviolence would not protect most people from a policeman's billy club. Ironically police often hustled her away from the site of any demonstration before they started swinging their clubs. They didn't want photos of a famous young girl with a bloodied nose broadcast around the world.

Still, she resolved, "It was no good saying that 'nonviolence works, up to a point.' That only meant that when things got too difficult or the activist was threatened with punishment, or was not attaining victory fast enough, it was time to switch to something more expedient."[9] Joan aimed to make nonviolence a principle for living, not merely a tactical method for achieving change. She and her friends ran the institute for four years.

In 1966 Joan continued her work with Martin Luther King, Jr. In the town of Grenada, Mississippi, she joined King in rallies and marches to integrate the public schools. Arm in arm, she and King marched with black elementary schoolchildren. This day, too, the children were turned away by a line of policemen who had been alerted to the march. But because Joan and Martin Luther King, Jr. were there, the event was televised, and the whole world could see it.

Meanwhile the United States began paying a steeper price for its involvement in Vietnamese affairs. By early 1967 an estimated 1,750 planes had been lost in the war. More than 6,600 American soldiers had been killed and over 37,000 wounded.

By spring, 427,000 Americans were fighting halfway around the world—and in New York City's Central Park, 300,000 young men and women demonstrated to end the United States' involvement in Vietnam. More than 175 young men threw their draft cards into a bonfire, and 20,000 people left the park to march through New York streets shouting, "Hell, no, we won't go!"

Joan began 1967 with her first concert tour of Japan. She had anticipated some difficulties in communicating with her audience, since she didn't speak Japanese. But these difficulties took a strange and sinister turn. Before each concert, her interpreter, a man named Takasaki, gave a five-minute speech that seemed to dampen the enthusiasm of her listeners. They weren't responding to the comments and polite remarks Joan tried to make between songs. An assistant to the interpreter explained that Takasaki was merely telling people not to smoke in the hall. Joan didn't believe this.

The troubles with Takasaki grew worse through the tour. Finally Joan met another Japanese man who listened to Takasaki's speech and told Joan that it contained nothing about smoking. Instead, Takasaki was telling listeners, "This girl has a lovely voice. You should listen to her sing, but as far as her politics goes, she doesn't know what she's talking about. She's innocent and young, and she came here to sing to the people, not to talk. So, simply ignore what she has to say."[10]

Joan was amazed. Why would this man make her look so foolish to her fans? One month later, the *New York Times* reported that Takasaki claimed that before Joan arrived in Japan, he had been approached by an American who said he was employed by the U.S. Central Intelligence Agency (CIA). This man knew Takasaki worked for two months every year in the United States and that he needed a visa to do this. According to Takasaki, the man said Takasaki would have trouble obtaining any more visas if he didn't change the meanings whenever Joan made any political statements on stage. Frightened, Takasaki agreed. After the article appeared, the United States government denied that any such thing had ever happened.

In her music and her life, Joan was setting impossibly high standards for herself. But with every step toward perfection, she was reminded of how human she was. She became very spiritual, listening to Gregorian chants and praying every day. Only when she wanted to did she go touring. In 1965 she gave only twenty concerts. But *TIME* magazine reported two years later that she was making as much as $8,500 per concert. This money, plus the royalties from record sales, enabled her to give away much of her earnings to groups she considered worthwhile. She also gave many free, fund-raising concerts for schools and peace groups.

Even though Joan was giving away much of the money she earned, she felt guilty about having more possessions than many other people.

Finally, Joan began to realize how much she enjoyed worldly pleasures, such as her house and clothes. And even if she allowed herself to have some fun now and then, she seemed to have forgotten how.

Fortunately for Joan, an international pop star has plenty

of opportunities to relearn. Traveling through Europe on a concert tour, she went shopping for clothes in Paris and Italy. She went horseback riding with an Austrian count. She met new and interesting men who took her dancing. She learned how to mix work and fun.

Joan's records had relied for their appeal almost entirely on the choices of songs and the quality of her singing. The arrangements were simple, the instrumental backing usually limited to one or two guitars. But in 1967 Joan released what many people feel was her most musically ambitious album to date. Simply entitled *Joan*, the album combined traditional folk songs with efforts from the best modern pop composers, such as Paul Simon, Donovan, the Beatles, and the French singer Jacques Brel.

More important, Joan hired a classical composer named Peter Schickele to write arrangements for an orchestra to support many of the songs. When Joan sang "Annabel Lee," the poem by Edgar Allan Poe set to music, Schickele's arrangement of bells shimmered and glistened around Joan's voice, creating an other-worldly effect. When she sang Brel's antiwar song, "The Dove," trumpets soared as dramatically as her voice.

Another highlight of the album was "Children of Darkness," written by Richard Farina, the husband of Joan's sister Mimi. The words and music are simple and Joan sings it simply. But behind her Schickele placed a groaning chorus of oboes, bassoons, and other woodwinds that invite listeners to imagine windswept nights on lonely Scottish moors. The effect was stunning and Joan showed the world that imaginative arrangements could make a wonderful singer sound even better.

In 1967 Joan plunged into another new adventure. Before the year was out, she would meet a new and special man— and she would marry him.

Chapter 6

NONVIOLENT SOLDIERS

"Oooooh, Mama. Ah'm down. They doin' it to me. An'm *way* down. I wanna see mah kids. An I don't *never* cry. But I b'lieve I'm gone have to today!"[1] And with that a tough, black dope addict folded herself into the arms of Joan Baez's mother and cried.

Joan, Senior, whom the black ladies at California's Santa Rita Prison all called "Mama," patted the woman's head, kissed her on the forehead, and said softly, but angrily, "Yeah. It's all pretty rotten, isn't it? Just plain stinking."[2]

In late 1967 "Mama and Joan Junior" had been arrested at a demonstration supporting the young men who refused to be drafted into the United States armed forces. The Baez women were sentenced to forty-five days in the women's section of Santa Rita Prison, but prison authorities released them after only two weeks because officials wanted to avoid the press conference Joan and her mother had planned for their original release date.

Prison officers also wanted to avoid the commotion of longer-term inmates saying their good-byes to the Baez women. So the officers didn't tell Joan and her mother they were going home until a half hour before they were released.

No fools, the Baezes took their time ironing clothes and distributing all their candy, skin lotion, and stamps, to give the prison grapevine time to work. Joan recalls, "Within fifteen minutes our most beloved and devoted friends made it through two locked doors . . . to the ironing room to embrace us and kiss us goodbye, and then to vanish down the starched but internally crumbling hallways of Santa Rita."[3]

This was Joan and her mother's second visit to Santa Rita. During their first stay in October, for ten days, Joan saw a man wearing a cowboy hat and a smile she thought was one of the sweetest in the world. His eyes were a shade she called "unfair blue." He was an unlikely looking inmate because he resembled an older version of the clean-cut kid who happily helps little old ladies across the street. Joan arranged to meet him in the prison cage, a little stall for visiting between the men's and women's sections.

Joan's original guesses about David Harris were accurate. In high school David had won "Boy of the Year" honors, along with trophies for debating and athletics. At Stanford University he was president of the student body. Now he was helping to lead a loose collection of antiwar groups called The Resistance. This movement aimed to upset and ultimately destroy the United States military simply by refusing to cooperate with the Selective Service System, which operated the draft.

To Joan, David was bright and clumsy, handsome and

messy, bright and very lovable. He also was strong and sure of his purpose in life. "Maybe he's what I need," she told herself. "Someone I don't just crave because his hair falls a certain way and his lips have a cupid's curl."[4] They decided to see each other after they were released from jail.

Within weeks of their release, Joan and David were living together. But in February 1968, David was put on trial for refusing induction into the armed forces. He was found guilty and sentenced to three years in prison beginning that July. David accepted his fate calmly and even used it to promote his cause. He and Joan toured college campuses. Joan sang a song or two, then David spoke about The Resistance.

After knowing each other only three months, Joan and David realized they wanted to marry each other. Joan called her mother with the news, which somehow also reached the major newspapers. Prodded by front-page announcements of their marriage, Joan and David decided to make quick plans. Surrounded by friends and families, Joan and David were wed in March.

Joan and David moved to a quarter acre of land they called Struggle Mountain in the Los Altos Hills. Most of their time was spent on college campuses, singing and speaking. David encouraged a humane society and he told students to work to improve people's lives.

Joan also talked to young people as she sang. Revolution,

she said, was not "name-calling, violence or guns," but "changing people's minds and hearts."[5] Asked if she was a pacifist, she replied that she was a "non-violent soldier who chooses to be a fighter, but not to use weapons."[6]

With their passionately held beliefs and a prison sentence looming in their future, life was intense and exciting for Joan and David. But it was hardly perfect. For all his genuine friendliness and skill at speaking to large groups, David was a private man, while Joan loved to trumpet her personal news and views to the world at large. During one of their speaking tours, Joan told David she was pregnant. Then she relayed the news to a concert audience at San Jose State. David was not pleased.

Next, Joan had her shoulder-length hair cut short. This act severed a link to her past life as an innocent, folk-singing maiden. Joan was preparing herself for motherhood. But again, David was upset. "You cut your hair off without asking me!"[7] he cried when he first saw her.

Before they married, Joan had warned David that she could be terribly strong-willed, possessive, and demanding. At these times her friends often called her "Queenie" (usually to her face). Now at times, Queenie found David's politics too rigid to accommodate romance. When she wanted him to take her out to dinner, spend money, and generally make a fuss over her, he would reply that being served in a restaurant was hopelessly materialistic and old-fashioned (in his words, "counterrevolutionary"). Joan continued her visits to a psychiatrist, trying to change roles from Queenie to "Wife."

On July 15, 1969 a sheriff and an assistant arrived at Struggle Mountain to take David to prison. He and Joan welcomed them with offers of coffee and juice and home-made bread, which they declined. David said his good-byes to friends and hugged Joan. Embarrassed by everyone's friendliness, the sheriff handcuffed David and drove away with him so fast that he didn't notice the RESIST THE DRAFT sticker that one of Joan's friends had placed on his bumper.

Everyone laughed for a moment. Then Joan prepared herself to be alone. Fortunately David would only have to serve twenty months of his three-year sentence. But during that time, life would change dramatically for the nation's most famous nonviolent soldiers.

Joan spent much of her pregnancy touring and singing. One reporter described her New York City concert as "a reunion of people with shared feelings and experiences who needed a boost in morale. . . . She spoke to the crowd of her jailed husband and of the draft-resistance movement as though she were addressing an old friend." While her songs were often sad spirituals and ballads, said the reporter, "the dominant message was one of keeping up hope in difficult times."[8] When Joan invited the audience to join her in singing her final song, "We Shall Overcome," the audience rose in unison, as if for the national anthem.

That summer Joan also appeared at Woodstock, the first of the great outdoor pop concerts. Pregnant and very much against taking drugs under any conditions, Joan felt somewhat out of place in the sloppy, drug-happy crowd that poured onto a small farm in upstate New York for three days of fun and music. And while performers like The Who and Jimi Hendrix smashed their guitars on stage and assaulted their listeners with electrical storms of sound, Joan was content to sing her songs of peace and harmony with only an acoustical guitar to support her. But she loved singing to an entire city of more than 250,000 young people.

Joan had always displayed to her public a face of unquenchable optimism. Now buoyed even further by the excitement of her coming child, she journeyed to Nashville, Tennessee. There she recorded two important record albums—actually three records' full of music—within an amazing four days. *David's Album*, a collection of country-and-western ballads and spirituals, conveyed a message of hope to her fans, and to the husband who could not be with her.

Even more amazing is the two-record set Joan recorded by reaching back to her past life with Bob Dylan. Called *Any Day Now*, the album contains nothing but Dylan songs. Typically, Joan avoided his more bitter or issue-oriented songs. Instead, she chose songs that focused on people, with strong lyrics and memorable melodies, which Dylan himself often garbled with his nasal, toneless manner of singing.

Joan says *Any Day Now* was one of the easiest albums she ever recorded. She spread sheet music all over the floor of the Nashville studio, shut her eyes and pointed, and sang whichever song came up. Backing her was a small, but superb, group of studio musicians. Even today, the songs sound as sad or playful or passionate or haunting as Joan meant them to sound in 1968. Many fans say that *Any Day Now* is one of the best Dylan albums Bob Dylan never made. It's an excellent introduction to Dylan's songs for anyone who has never heard them.

One day, as David's prison term was nearing the end, he received a phone call from Joan. She told him she had given birth to a baby boy and named him Gabriel.

Joan loved being a mother to Gabe. But she did not welcome the idea of sharing Gabe with her husband. Before David was released, Joan had an affair with another man. And when David returned from prison to press conferences, parties, and the good wishes of his friends and supporters, Joan knew that she considered Gabe to be hers alone and merely on loan to her husband. Finally Joan realized that as Gabe's father, David "had rights to him and to his time and to his love," Joan recollects, and "I was furious."[9]

"We didn't split up over Gabe, or over the affair I'd had, though it had been quite real and not a passing fancy. We didn't split up over politics. We split up, when we did, because I couldn't breathe, and I couldn't try anymore to be a wife, and because I belonged alone, which is how I have been since then, with occasional interruptions . . . I cannot possibly live in the same house with anyone. . . . I am made to live alone."[10]

Cynics might say that in the battle between Queenie and Wife, Queenie had won. But Joan remained close to David because she never stopped respecting him and because they both loved Gabe. David moved a half-hour away and Gabe went back and forth between them.

They managed parenthood "by fighting and crying with frustration, and tugging and pulling at Gabe's loyalties, and then breaking down and seeing how miserably we were behaving, and then trying to learn to trust each other," she says. "That trust came, little by little, and with an enormous amount of work. And we worked because we loved Gabe. . . . We did our absolute best."[11]

In 1969 Joan made an album of country songs, *One Day at a Time*. Then in 1971 she released *Blessed Are. . . .* , the first album to contain several songs she had written. She wrote about David, about traveling through Europe with Gabe on her hip, and about the many strange and funny experiences in her life. "Some songs came fast and suddenly, some in the middle of the night. Some were laborious efforts," Joan recalls. "They were very personal, and in my opinion none rated much over a five. But writing gave me a satisfaction I'd not felt from singing other people's work."[12]

In 1970 her record company also released a two-album set of already recorded songs called *The First Ten Years*. This was an appropriate move because both Joan and Maynard Solomon, one of her first friends and supporters in the music business, agreed that it was time to part company. Like her divorce from David, Joan's split from Vanguard Records was accomplished with mutual affection and respect and pain.

For many years, Vanguard Records continued to repackage and rerelease Joan's original songs. These albums would often sell more copies around the world than the albums of new songs Joan made with other record companies. In the 1970s times were changing once more, and for Joan's career, the times ahead were going to be tough.

In 1972 Joan directly confronted the reality of the war she had protested for so long. A group of North Vietnamese called the Committee for Solidarity with the American People invited Joan to visit Hanoi, the capital of America's enemy in the war, North Vietnam. For thirteen days in December, Joan joined three other Americans, a lawyer, a minister, and an antiwar activist, to discover how people lived under daily bombings by American B-52 aircraft.

At first her visit to Hanoi was filled with predictable meetings, friendly dinners, and quiet tours. Joan carried a tape recorder with her to capture local sounds and songs. On her third night, her hosts were showing the group a film about the war when the hotel lights suddenly went out. Then a siren sounded. U.S. bombers were approaching.

All the hotel's guests hurried out the rear door to an air-raid shelter, where they waited. When the first bombs hit the city, they shook the shelter and Joan found herself shaking just as badly. After several minutes of continous bombing the sound of planes got softer. Perhaps this terrible experience was over.

The next bomb exploded before anyone in the shelter even heard the planes. Joan took a deep breath and felt like vomiting. The "carpet bombing" raining down on them was "like thunder, the kind of thunder that rolls and rolls when you see purple lightning like strobe-lit twigs hurled into the air at the edge of a desert horizon," Joan said later. "We rode out the minutes. . . . I realized with shame and horror that to pray for the planes to go away was to pray that they would drop their bombs somewhere else."[13]

Finally the bombing stopped and Joan returned to her room, only to leave moments later for the shelter when the bombing started again. This night there would be ten air raids in all. By dawn, she was no less scared, but a veteran. And she began to take her tape recorder with her, to capture the incredible noise and fear around her.

The bombing continued for the next eleven days Joan

remained in Hanoi. Joan saw dead people lying by the road and bomb craters thirty feet wide. With her recorder she taped the sirens, the bombs, antiaircraft guns, children laughing, Vietnamese singing, herself singing to frightened people in the shelter, and midnight Mass at a local church on Christmas Eve.

The most heart-wrenching moment occurred one morning when Joan saw a woman bending low to the ground over a bomb crater. She was singing to herself as she hobbled back and forth. Joan thought she was singing a song of joy that her family was still alive after the night's bombing. But as Joan and an interpreter drew closer to the woman, her song became a moan. The interpreter said she was looking for her son who lay somewhere under their feet, packed into a grave of mud.

Joan was never so happy to arrive home as she was after her trip to Hanoi. She had recorded fifteen hours of tape, including the woman's terrible song of grief. In 1973 she released an album of poems, sounds, and songs called *Where Are You Now, My Son?* She called it her "gift to the Vietnamese people, and my prayer of thanks for being alive."[14]

America's involvement in Vietnam ended in January 1973. All American forces withdrew from South Vietnam. The war had killed more than 58,000 Americans and wounded another 155,000 men and women. Over a million Vietnamese civilians had been killed. Within another two years, South Vietnam surrendered to North Vietnamese forces, and the entire country fell under Communist rule.

Chapter 7

TIMELESS BUT NOT TIMELY

"No carabinieri!" Joan shouted in her best broken Italian as the policeman raced on foot toward the young man. He had jumped the fence to L'Arena, a soccer stadium in Milan, Italy, where Joan was performing for thirty thousand people. She first saw the gate-crasher from her raised platform stage when a group of people sitting near her on the soccer field rose up in unison and started screaming.

As the policeman gave chase, Joan shouted again into the microphone for him to stop. When he did, walking away in disgust and embarrassment, students representing Communist and anarchist political groups gave a victory roar and greeted the gate-crasher as a hero. More conservative students on the field, and an older crowd in the bleachers, maintained an unfriendly silence.

Order was restored until Joan began a song called "The Ghetto," which twice mentioned the word "revolution." Groups of revolution-minded students began screaming and running for her platform, which was only four feet off the ground. As they jumped onto the stage, someone ripped out the electrical cords, leaving Joan with no microphone to calm the crowd.

Without thinking, she raised her guitar into the air to keep it safe. But this action only seemed to inflame the crowd more. Joan was in danger of being crushed in the onslaught.

Somehow a friend reached her, picked her up in his arms, pushed people out of the way, and carried her down make-shift stairs to safety. Later, another friend told her that by holding her guitar in the air out of reach, she had provoked her audience with a prize to capture, like a flag in the midst of battle. The higher she held her guitar, the more people wanted to claim it.

Outside the United States, dramatic behavior was becoming increasingly common at Joan's concerts as the 1970s began. Throughout Europe, Asia, and Latin America, music and politics remained so closely entwined that a politically minded performer such as Joan continued to stir strong passions, both for and against her.

But as the United States involvement in Vietnam wound to a close, the musical tastes of young Americans began to change again. Much of the music remained as simply orchestrated and richly melodic as Joan's songs. But new performers who attracted the most attention—such as James Taylor, Joni Mitchell, Jackson Browne, and Carole King—preferred to turn inward with their music. Rather than singing about the injustice experienced by others, these performers sang about their own difficulties in dealing with a world that was often hostile and uncaring. The emotional turmoil presented on their records touched millions of sensitive and troubled young people.

Ironically just as Joan and her music began to fall behind the times, she had her first and only hit record. In 1972 after she left Vanguard Records and signed with a company called A & M, Vanguard released a single called "The Night They Drove Old Dixie Down." A pleasant but unspectacular remake of another group's song, "Dixie" quickly reached the top ten. Since then, no single of Joan's has done nearly as well.

Through the early 1970s, Joan found that her most memorable moments as a performer usually took place outside the United States. Singing at a university stadium in Venezuela, for example, she once more became caught in a battle of wills. Again, many of her listeners were politically active and loudly willing to defy authority. As Joan began to sing, students left their bleacher seats to sit before her in the stadium field. Everyone knew this action was against university rules.

As Joan began her second song, the electricity went dead. A chorus of boos went up. Time passed and no one restored the electricity. Rumors circulated that the university's president, who was in the crowd, had ordered the sound off until the students returned to their seats.

Joan's manager convinced the president to restore electricity for one minute, so Joan could announce that the students must return to their seats. Joan thought the rule was ridiculous. But could she risk allowing a riot like the one in Italy to happen again?

She made her decision. In Spanish just as halting as her Italian, she thanked the president for restoring the electricity. She told him the crowd was causing her no problem, and she dedicated the next song to him. "If you like the song," she announced, ". . . let me know by leaving the sound on."[1] She sang, the sound and the students remained as they were, and everyone had a terrific time.

In another country, her decision to sing one song—and the power and symbolism of that song—caused a nationwide reaction. And this time, not everyone benefited from Joan's decision. She first appeared in Spain one year after the death of a powerful dictator, Generalissimo Francisco Franco. After forty years of struggle against Franco, a government of liberals, Communists, and Socialists had come to power.

Two years before appearing in Spain, in 1974, Joan had released an album of all Spanish-language songs, called *Gracias a La Vida* ("Thanks to Life"). It had sold very well in Spanish-speaking countries. But in politically sensitive Spain, the album had been released with two songs missing. One of them, *No Nos Moveran* ("We Shall Not Be Moved"), was an anthem of the anti-Franco resistance and had not been sung openly in Spain for four decades. Even a year after Franco's death, no one dared to sing this song in public.

Joan agreed to appear on a television show to be broadcast throughout Spain. She memorized introductions in Spanish and selected three songs, two of them Spanish. Before appearing on stage, she told the producer of her choices. The first song was *No Nos Moveran.*

> Unido en la lucha (Together in the struggle)
> Unidos en la vita (Together in life)
> Unidos en la Muerta (Together in death)
> No nos moveran (We shall not be moved)

Joan didn't know how her audience in the studio or at home would react. She says it was as if a spell or perhaps a protective layer of silence had been broken. By the end of the song, cameramen and audience members alike were brushing away tears and rising to join her in the chorus. Apparently, all over Spain, people were reacting to "No Nos Moveran" with hugs and tears.

The producer of the show was fired. He knew what Joan was planning and his decision not to interfere cost him his job. In Spain music has a power not even Joan could always control.

For years Joan had used her talents to promote goals such as the end of wars and the arms race. All along she knew these goals could never be achieved in her lifetime. This realization caused her to look for work that produced more tangible results. And in 1973 she found it.

A friend introduced Joan to Amnesty International. This organization works around the world for the release of "prisoners of conscience." Amnesty works for anyone imprisoned for reasons of ethnic origins or religious or political beliefs and persons who have never used violence or supported the use of violence. With the support of both right and left-wing governments, many prisoners of conscience were being apprehended and taken to jail. Some were beaten with rubber hoses, shocked with electrical wires, or suffered other forms of torture.

Amnesty International already had offices in London and New York City. Joan was asked to help organize an office in California. For a full year, Joan threw herself into the task. She traveled up and down the West Coast, raising funds, meeting with newspaper editors, going to private homes to give talks on how to form an Amnesty group. A group was expected to register with Amnesty's London office and meet at least once a month. The group would be sent names of people Amnesty felt were prisoners of conscience and the groups would begin a letter-writing campaign to the authorities in charge of the prisoner asking them to release him or her from prison. Prodded by Joan and others, Amnesty International groups began to spring up along the West Coast.

"I decided to work directly with Amnesty until the day when any newspaper or radio talk show I approached would know what Amnesty International was, and when the facts, coming from London, were no longer disputed," she says. "It took only a year."[2]

Years later Joan was asked if she ever became discouraged in her pursuit for world peace. She said no. "One suffers under a marvelous illusion that as long as you're working, something's still happening," she replied. "Although I joke about having no illusions, that may be the one that I hang on to. . . . I don't deny the possibility of hope. Action is the antidote to despair."[3]

By 1975 the folk music that had propelled Joan to stardom was rapidly becoming old-fashioned. If she wanted to prosper, Joan needed to make an incredibly strong album. And in 1975 she did. But for the first time she did it by making compromises for commercial success.

The album's producer insisted that Joan include songs that were peppy and cheerful, or at least familiar to young audiences. Joan realized that "up" songs didn't come naturally to her, unless she was singing with someone else's band, having a drink or two, or singing in Spanish. But she gave in, without fighting, because she wanted to make a record that succeeded both musically and commercially.

By following her producer's advice to "lighten up," Joan produced one of her most varied and enjoyable albums,

Diamonds and Rust. A listener today would be hard-pressed to understand how Joan could have objected to many of the songs by Jackson Browne, Stevie Wonder, Janis Ian, and the Allman Brothers. She delivers the songs with great energy and feeling, so they don't seem slight or superficial at all.

For the first time on this album, Joan also began playing the synthesizer and composing music for its own sake, rather than as a vehicle for words. When a fragment of free-form jazz she composed was warmly received by her band, she went home and wrote verses for it. "Children and All That Jazz" is a funny look at the difficulties of keeping up with Gabe who was then eight years old.

Not surprising, the presence of her "mystic brother," Bob Dylan, also fills *Diamonds and Rust*. Earlier that year, Joan had joined the Rolling Thunder Tour, a traveling circus of singers and musicians that Dylan had organized to barnstorm the United States. To open the second half of each show, Joan and Bob appeared on stage with identical guitars, flowered cowboy hats, vests, pants, and long scarves. An excellent mimic, Joan even copied Bob's voice and hand gestures. Everyone had been amused.

Now in the studio Joan once more found inspiration from Bob Dylan. She wrote "Winds of the Old Days," thanking Dylan for "writing the best songs" and "righting a few wrongs." She sang his "Simple Twist of Fate" with terrific energy as a flat-out, rock-and-roll number. She capped the album with its title tune, "Diamonds and Rust." Backing herself on both acoustical guitar and synthesizer, Joan delivered a haunting tribute to her early days with Dylan. After many years and repeated listenings, this song can still bring chills to a listener. *Diamonds and Rust* became one of the standout recordings of 1975.

Unfortunately her career troubles now became more pronounced. In 1976 Joan made what she now calls "the stupidest 'career move' of my life"[4] by again changing record companies. She joined a small label called Portrait, for whom she recorded two albums. For a number of reasons the company refused to support her albums with money for advertising and promotion. Joan probably did not help her cause by having a political argument about Israel with the company president. Both albums sold dismally.

After being nurtured for decades on sensitive treatment by executives such as Vanguard's Solomon brothers, Joan was deeply hurt by her new record company's lack of support. "I simply did not grasp the fact that I was no longer considered a 'hot item,'" she says. With some pain and humiliation, she realized that "though I might be timeless in the world of music, at least in the United States I was no longer *timely*."[5]

To make matters worse, Joan began to acknowledge a problem she'd been having for three years. She had built her career as an "achingly pure soprano." Now her voice was failing her. It had happened so much that she was no longer a soprano, and a constant tickle in her throat made it difficult for her to hit any high notes at all.

She had resisted friends' suggestions to get help for her voice. Stubbornly she refused to see herself as anything but a natural songstress. Finally she realized she was being stubborn. She went to a voice instructor named Robert Bernard, who told her that after age forty gravity took over the body and affected the vocal chords. With vocal exercises, much like aerobics, she could repair the damage.

The vocal exercises were humiliating. One time, she said, "somebody in a hotel called down to the manager and said there was an animal trapped in the room next door. That's how attractive they [the exercises] are."[6]

She began doing her exercises at least twenty minutes a day. And gradually she recovered the vocal power and control she once had. She plans to continue the exercises until the day she stops performing.

In 1979 Joan appeared at a concert in Germany that pointed the way toward her future. As an experiment, she agreed to sing in a rock show between Frank Zappa and Genesis. She would sing for forty minutes as the sun was setting.

This was a rock-and-roll show with "55,000 very happy, doped-out kids,"[7] she remembers. They had come to dance, get drunk, and pass out. Unknown to her, the promoters backstage were taking bets on how long it would take for the unruly crowd to resoundingly boo Joan off the stage. Even she thought her appearance would be a major disaster.

For the first twenty minutes, Joan worked very hard to make contact with her audience. Her first song flopped because no one recognized it. She cut it short and began to talk to the crowd about war and peace and human rights. "And I brought them down to earth, which is where people have to land if they're ever going to think,"[8] she remembers.

And slowly, she remembers, "This *thing* began to happen."[9] She sang her next song, and groups of listeners on the sides began to chant, "Sitzen, sitzen!" ("sit down, sit down") to the rocking, drinking crowd up front. Then a Bob Dylan song started many of them clapping along in rhythm. When she began singing the folk classic "Where Have All the Flowers Gone?" in German, the crowd roared in approval.

The sound system was excellent and Joan's restored voice carried across the river from the concert stage, where hundreds more young Germans stood along a riverbank, listening. "By the end of forty minutes, they were calling for 'Blowin' in the Wind,' 'We Shall Overcome.' They were weeping, they were lighting candles," she recalls. "I meant something to them—I represented the Sixties, that was clear. I stood for John Lennon, Bob Dylan, people they needed as heroes. They are fresh out of heroes in the Eighties."[10]

When Joan left the stage, the crowd roared and stamped. Then from backstage, everyone heard the sound of beer cans clattering off the curtains and flying in every direction. Joan was not being booed. The crowd was saying they wanted her back.

Inspired by her triumph, she wrote a song to prepare young people—and herself—for the decade to come. She called the song "Children of the Eighties."

> We're children of the eighties and haven't we
> grown?
> We're tender as a lotus and tougher than stone,
> And the age of our innocence is somewhere in
> the garden. . .
> We like the music of the sixties
> We think that era must have been nifty,
> The Rolling Stones, the Beatles, and the Doors,
> Flower children, Woodstock, and the war,
> Dirty scandals, cover-ups, and more.
> Ah, but it's getting harder to deceive us. . .
>
> We are children of the eighties.[11]

Chapter 8

BASH ON, REGARDLESS

At the end of the 1970s, Joan was anxious to put her memories of Vietnam behind her. For her, as for most Americans, the war was over when United States troops had pulled out of Vietnam six years earlier. But for the Vietnamese people, Joan now discovered, the war was far from finished. According to two Vietnamese men who visited Joan in 1979, the victorious Communist government was behaving just as brutally toward its citizens as the United States-supported South Vietnamese government had behaved.

Joan had campaigned vigorously against the United States involvement in Vietnam. She had visited Hanoi, which was now being accused of mistreating its own people. She had made a record album that detailed the Vietnamese suffering under American bombs. Many Americans had branded Joan a Communist for her actions. To this, Joan replied that she never blindly placed her trust in any one form of government. "For some Godforsaken reason," she once said, "I was given the gift of not having an ideology."[1]

Now she felt compelled to demonstrate that she meant what she always said. She formed a study group of friends, who began researching and questioning the two men's accusations. The group talked with diplomats, reporters, exiles, and refugees from Vietnam. They talked with Communists and supporters of the United States.

What Joan's group discovered was grim. The Communists in Hanoi did indeed seem bent on destroying their own resources. Jails in Vietnam were overflowing with thousands of "detainees," perhaps as many as 200,000 people locked up solely because they opposed the new government. Many of these people were being shipped to reeducation centers, where they were tortured and fed starvation diets. Some were even used as human mine detectors, clearing live mine fields with their hands and feet.

Once more Joan decided to speak out. She wrote an open letter to the Socialist Republic of Vietnam, asking for an end to the imprisonment and torture. Then she began collecting signatures to support her position. Her group raised $53,000 to pay to print the letter in four major American newspapers.

During the weeks she spent gathering support, Joan realized that for many Americans the wounds of war were still fresh. Friends told her she was being manipulated by so-called Communists who were actually working for the United States. Others said she was betraying the Vietnamese people by criticizing their new government.

When the letter appeared, the Communist government

called its accusations untrue. All over America, prominent antiwar activists branded Joan foolish, naive, or a paid agent of the CIA. On the other extreme, Americans who had supported America's actions in Vietnam basically replied, "We told you so," and cynically called Joan and her supporters new-found humanitarians.

Joan's letter changed little in Vietnam. The imprisonment and torture of innocent citizens continued for years. But Joan felt it was important to do the right thing, even if it meant exposing herself to scathing criticism from people whose feelings and beliefs she had once shared.

That same year, Joan also became aware of the many people throughout Southeast Asia—in the countries of Laos, Thailand, and Cambodia—who were being forced off their land by continuing wars throughout the region. She decided that the American people must recognize the plight of these displaced refugees, just as Joan's two visitors had forced her to confront the situation in Vietnam.

With a few friends, Joan organized a trip to Southeast Asia. A team of refugee workers and newspaper reporters accompanied them. In the United States, Joan's activities were still considered newsworthy. Perhaps her presence in Laotian and Cambodian refugee camps would bring television crews whose films would appear on nightly American television.

Her first stop was northern Thailand, where thousands of

refugees came to hear Joan sing. Few if any of these people knew who Joan was or why she was there. But American TV networks knew. They sent cameramen to follow Joan and record the refugees' terrible stories of imprisonment and torture. They shot scenes of Joan holding children dressed in rags and on the verge of death.

Over the years Joan had learned that television and newspapers could be manipulated to serve her needs, and now Joan was using the media very skillfully. Once she was being interviewed by CBS when a rocket exploded nearby. She nearly jumped out of her skin with fright. But she immediately calmed herself because sounds of war almost guaranteed that the cameraman's footage would appear on the evening news in America.

Her trip had a few light moments. One song she performed regularly for refugee children was "I Love My Rooster." It was filled with sheep *baaaaa*'s, cow *mooo*'s, and other animal noises that made Joan feel like an idiot. But any child can understand it, and the song invariably provoked snickers and giggles.

Back home in California, Joan and her friends formed a group they called Humanitas. They launched a campaign that raised $1,250,000 in ten days over the Christmas holidays of 1979. A friend of Joan's returned to the refugee camps with the money, which she used to purchase food and medical supplies for the refugees.

When Joan's son Gabe reached junior high age, he told his mother that she was mentioned in his history book. Joan may have been flattered, but she also was determined not to to become an antique. She could change with the times. For example, as a younger woman Joan tended to become furious when well-meaning friends told her that her long hair, gladiator sandals, and bright, native blouses might put off potential supporters. She felt it was what one did that counted. But she soon learned.

"But it's a *style* that you either threaten people with or don't. . . . I'm going to sing for the French president's wife— she's willing to set up an organization that will fight for human rights in Afghanistan as well as El Salvador. That's a very important move. So when I visit her at the palace, I'll go dressed a certain way. . . . And when I go visiting the ghettoes in Venezuela, I'll go dressed another way. Wherever it is, you make the people you are with comfortable with what you have on—'cause they're not gonna be comfortable with what you have to say."[2]

The 1980s were filled with personal changes in Joan's life as well. When Gabe was twelve, Joan decided that he needed a firm male hand. David Harris had since remarried and his wife was expecting a child. Now Joan and David decided that Gabe would be raised by the Harrises.

Joan and David remained on good enough terms that she joined the new Harris family to cheer Gabe through important moments. When he was fifteen, Joan found herself in an odd role—standing on the sidelines of a football field at Gabe's prep school, near Boston, as Gabe played on the school team.

For a moment, Joan wondered if the high priestess of non-violence could possibly cheer as her son knocked other boys to the ground. But she was so proud of him that she couldn't help yelling with the rest of the crowd although she had no idea what the boys on the field were doing.

During the 1980s, Joan gradually reemerged as a singer and performer in the United States. Her appearance at Live Aid in 1985 started the ball rolling. That same year she joined several folk singers (including her sister Mimi Farina) in a three-night concert to celebrate the twenty-fifth anniversary of Club 47. This was a special moment for Joan, because at this Cambridge, Massachusetts, club Joan first sang professionally to the tiny, half-filled room for $10 a night.

In 1986 Joan joined the "Conspiracy of Hope" concert tour with U2, Sting, and Peter Gabriel to raise funds for Amnesty International during its twenty-fifth anniversary year. In 1987 she published her autobiography, *And A Voice to Sing With*, the product of five years' work.

Speaking of Dreams, Joan's first album of new songs in several years, was released in 1989. As always, her musical interests span the globe. One song that she wrote, "China," pays tribute to the brave students who died in the 1989 Beijing demonstrations. She sings of Central America in a lovely ballad called "El Salvador," written by Greg Copeland. A catchy pop tune called "Hand to Mouth," written by George Michael, manages to convey a solid message about helping poor and homeless people anywhere we find them. From first song to last, Joan sounds as fresh and vibrant as ever.

"If you look around [at] the state of the world, you see that it's absolutely grim," she said once, in describing thirty years in the public eye. "But then, there's this wonderful British expression I use: 'Bash on, regardless!' . . . It means go and be quiet and try to get some direction. It means stay informed. . . . [It means] you don't stop because it's grim.[3]

"When somebody says to me—which they do like every five years—'How does it feel to be over the hill,' my response is, 'I'm just heading up the mountain.'"[4]

In 1986 Joan sings at a concert to raise money for Amnesty International.

APPENDIX

RECORDINGS OF JOAN BAEZ

Joan Baez (1960)
Joan Baez/Volume 2 (1961)
Joan Baez in Concert (1962)
Joan Baez in Concert/Part Two (1963)
Joan Baez/5 (1964)
Farewell, Angelina (1965)
Noel (1966)
Joan (1967)
Baptism: A Journey Through Our Time (1968)
Any Day Now (1968)
David's Album (1969)
One Day at a Time (1969)
Joan Baez—The First Ten Years (1970)
Blessed Are . . . (1971)
Carry It On (soundtrack) (1971)
The Joan Baez Ballad Book (1972)
Come From the Shadows (1972)
Where Are You Now, My Son? (1973)
Hits/Greatest and Others (1973)
Gracias a La Vida (1974)
Contemporary Ballad Book (1974)
Diamonds & Rust (1975)
From Every Stage (1976)
Gulf Winds (1976)
Lovesong Album (1976)
Blowin' Away (1977)
Best of Joan C. Baez (1977)
Honest Lullaby (1979)
Very Early Joan (1982)
Recently (1987)
Diamonds & Rust in the Bullring (1989)
Speaking of Dreams (1989)

PUBLICATIONS BY JOAN BAEZ

Joan Baez Songbook (1964)
Daybreak (1968)
Coming Out (with David Harris) (1971)
And Then I Wrote . . . (songbook) (1979)
And a Voice To Sing With: A Memoir (1987)

NOTES

Chapter 1

1. Peter Hillmore, *World-Wide Concert Book: Live Aid* (London: Sidgwick & Jackson Ltd., 1985: New Jersey: The Unicorn Publishing House, 1985), 42.
2. Joan Baez, *And a Voice to Sing With* (New York: Summit Books, 1987), 357-58.
3. "Concert," *Philadelphia Daily News* (July 15, 1985), 12.

Chapter 2

1. "Joan Baez," *Rolling Stone* (November 5th-December 10th, 1987), 163.
2. Joan Baez, *Daybreak* (New York: Avon Books, 1966, 1968), 33.
3. Ibid.
4. Ibid., 52.
5. Joan Baez, *And a Voice to Sing With* (New York: Summit Books, 1987), 24.
6. Ibid., 23.
7. Ibid., 24.
8. Ibid., 25.
9. Ibid., 30.
10. Ibid., 29.
11. Ibid., 35.
12. Ibid., 36.
13. Ibid., 44.
14. Ibid., 40.
15. Ibid., 33.

Chapter 3

1. Joan Baez, *And a Voice to Sing With*, (New York: Summit Books, 1987), 50.
2. Ibid., 53.
3. Ibid.
4. Ibid., 58.
5. "Joan Baez: The Rolling Stone Interview," *Rolling Stone*, (April 14, 1983), 18.
6. Baez, *And a Voice to Sing With*, 55.
7. Ibid., 58.
8. Ibid., 60.
9. Ibid.

10. Ibid., 61.
11. Ibid., 65.
12. "Joan Baez: The Rolling Stone Interview," *Rolling Stone*, (April 14, 1983), 18.

Chapter 4

1. Joan Baez, *And a Voice to Sing With*, (New York: Summit Books, 1978), 70.
2. Ibid., 84.
3. Ibid.
4. Ibid., 104.
5. "Sibyl with Guitar," *Time*, (November 23, 1962), 54.
6. Ibid., 56.
7. Ibid., 54.
8. "Joan Baez: The Rolling Stone Interview," *Rolling Stone*, (April 14, 1983), 18.
9. Baez, *And a Voice to Sing With*, 115.
10. "The 100 Best Singles of the Last 25 Years," *Rolling Stone*, (September 8th, 1988), 63.
11. Baez, *And a Voice to Sing With*, 85.
12. Ibid., 89-90.
13. Ibid., 85.

Chapter 5

1. Joan Baez, *And a Voice to Sing With*, (New York: Summit Books, 1978), 120.
2. Ibid., 86-87.
3. Richard Farina, "Baez and Dylan: A Generation Singing Out," *Mademoiselle*, (August 1964), 338.
4. Baez, *And a Voice to Sing With*, 96.
5. Ibid.
6. Ibid., 124.
7. Ibid.
8. Ibid., 126.
9. Ibid.
10. Ibid., 142.

Chapter 6

1. Joan Baez, *Daybreak*, (New York: Avon Books, 1966, 1968), 41.

2. Ibid.
3. Ibid., 44.
4. Joan Baez, *And a Voice to Sing With*, (New York: Summit Books, 1987), 147.
5. "Summer's Gain, Autumn's Loss," *Saturday Review*, (August 23, 1969), 55.
6. Ibid.
7. Baez, *And a Voice to Sing With*, 155.
8. "Garden Gathering," from The Talk of the Town, *The New Yorker*, (August 23, 1969), 23.
9. Baez, *And a Voice to Sing With*, 159.
10. Ibid., 160.
11. Ibid., 162.
12. Ibid., 167.
13. Ibid., 204.
14. Ibid., 225.

Chapter 7
1. Joan Baez, *And a Voice to Sing With*, (New York: Summit Books, 1987), 228.
2. Ibid., 183.
3. "Joan Baez: The Rolling Stone Interview," *Rolling Stone*, (April 14, 1983), 20.

4. Baez, *And a Voice to Sing With*, 293.
5. Ibid., 294-95.
6. "Joan Baez," *Rolling Stone*, (November 5th-December 10th, 1987), 164.
7. Joan Baez: "The Rolling Stone Interview," *Rolling Stone*, (April 14, 1983), 18.
8. Ibid.
9. Ibid.
10. Ibid.
11. "Children of the Eighties," by Joan Baez. Published by Gabriel Ear. Music, 1987.

Chapter 8
1. "Joan Baez: The Rolling Stone Interview," *Rolling Stone*, (April 14, 1983), 19.
2. Ibid., 20.
3. "Joan Baez," *Rolling Stone*, (November 5th-December 10th, 1987), 164.
4. "Joan Baez: The Rolling Stone Interview," *Rolling Stone*, (April 14, 1983), 20.

Joan Baez 1941-

1941   Joan Chandos Baez is born on January 9, the second child and second daughter of Joan and Albert Baez. Germany invades U.S.S.R. as World War II continues. British Royal Air Force bombs Nuremberg, Germany. Japanese bomb Pearl Harbor. U.S. and Britain declare war on Japan. Germany and Italy declare war on U.S. U.S. declares war on Germany and Italy. Japan captures the Philippines. Dacron is invented.

1942   U.S. transfers more than 100,000 Japanese-Americans to West Coast internment camps. Germans reach Stalingrad, U.S.S.R. The murder of millions of Jews in gas chambers begins. Mohandas K. Gandhi demands independence for India and is arrested.

1943   London, England, suffers new German attacks. German army surrenders at Stalingrad. Allied forces in North Africa are placed under General Dwight D. Eisenhower. U.S. forces regain islands in Pacific from Japanese. Winston Churchill, prime minister of Britain; Franklin D. Roosevelt, president of U.S.; and Joseph Stalin, Soviet dictator hold Teheran (Iran) conference. Allied "round-the-clock" bombing of Germany begins. Italy joins the Allied forces.

1944   Heavy German air raids on London. D-Day—Allies land on Normandy and liberate Antwerp, Brussels, and Paris. General Charles de Gaulle enters liberated Paris with the Free French Forces. U.S. troops land in Philippines. Franklin Roosevelt is elected for fourth term. Vietnam declares herself independent of France.

1945   Mimi Margharita Baez is born on April 30. Roosevelt dies and Vice-President Harry S. Truman becomes president of the U.S. Italian Fascist leader Benito Mussolini is killed by Italian partisans. Nazi leader Adolf Hitler commits suicide. Berlin surrenders to Soviets and Germany capitulates. VE (Victory in Europe) Day ends World War II in Europe. Churchill, Truman, and Stalin confer at Potsdam, Germany. U.S. drops atomic bombs on Hiroshima and Nagasaki in Japan. VJ (Victory over Japan) Day celebrated as Japan surrenders to end World War II. The United Nations (UN) comes into existence.

1946   United Nations (UN) General Assembly holds its first session in London. New York City becomes the permanent headquarters for the UN.

1947   *The Diary of Anne Frank* is published posthumously.

1948   In India, Mohandas K. Gandhi is assassinated. Truman is elected president of the U.S. The transistor is invented.

1950   The Korean War begins. Nelson Mandela, of South Africa, becomes president of the African National Congress (ANC) Youth League.

1951   The Baez family moves to Baghdad, Iraq, where Joan's passion for social justice is born.

1952   Joan begins guitar lessons. General Dwight D. Eisenhower is elected president of the U.S. Mandela is arrested for defying 11:00 P.M. curfew.

1953   Korean War ends. Mandela appears in court as a lawyer, while the ANC goes underground. Jonas Salk begins inoculating children with the polio vaccine he developed. U.S. Supreme Court rules that segregation by color in public schools is unconstitutional.

1955   In the United States, blacks in Montgomery, Alabama, organize a bus boycott.

1956   Eisenhower is reelected president of the U.S.

1957   U.S. Supreme Court declares that forcing blacks into "separate but equal" public schools is unconstitutional.

1958   The Baez family moves to Boston, Massachusetts. Joan begins singing in local coffeehouses.

1959   Joan Baez sings at the Gate of Horn in Chicago. During the summer she performs at the

Newport Jazz Festival in Newport, Rhode Island.

1960 John F. Kennedy is elected president of the U.S. In Sharpeville, South Africa, 69 anti-apartheid demonstrators are killed and almost 200 wounded. Laser beams are developed.

1961 Joan gives 20 concerts. U.S. Peace Corps is begun. Nonviolent peaceful protests for voter registration and an end to discrimination take place throughout the South. The Republic of South Africa becomes a nation and Nelson Mandela goes into hiding as he works for freedom causes.

1962 Joan makes concert tour of the South. U.S. military council established in South Vietnam.

1963 Joan gives concerts with Bob Dylan. The Reverend Martin Luther King, Jr. gives his "I Have a Dream" speech at the Lincoln Memorial in Washington, D.C. Joan Baez leads the singing. Nelson Mandela is tried for conspiracy. President Kennedy is assassinated; Vice-president Lyndon B. Johnson becomes president of the U.S. "The Great Train Robbery" succeeds in Britain.

1964 President Johnson pushes for passage of the Civil Rights Bill. U.S. becomes involved in fighting in Vietnam. In a protest against the Vietnam War, Joan Baez refuses to pay 60 percent of her federal income taxes. Martin Luther King, Jr. wins the Nobel Peace Prize. Mandela is sentenced to life imprisonment. Lyndon B. Johnson is elected president of the U.S.

1965 Voting Rights Act signed by President Johnson. Martin Luther King, Jr. leads 4,000 civil rights demonstrators in a march from Selma to Montgomery, Alabama. Joan founds Institute for the Study of Nonviolence, now called Resource Center for Nonviolence. U.S. involvement in Vietnam escalates.

1966 Joan joins Martin Luther King, Jr. in rallies and marches. Demonstrations against American involvement in Vietnam War occur.

1967 Thurgood Marshall becomes the first black Supreme Court justice. Joan makes concert tour of Japan. Joan and her mother are arrested at rally supporting young men who refused to be drafted. In the U.S. 50,000 persons demonstrate against the Vietnam War.

1968 Joan marries David Harris. Reverend King, Jr. is assassinated in Memphis. Senator Robert F. Kennedy is assassinated. President Johnson announces he will not run for reelection; most people attribute that decision to the Americans' feeling about the Vietnam War. Richard M. Nixon is elected president of the U.S.

1969 David Harris is sentenced to prison for resisting the draft. Joan appears at Woodstock, the first of the outdoor pop concerts. Joan and David have a son, Gabriel Earl. Hundreds of thousands of Americans demonstrate against the Vietnam War.

1970 In the U.S. student protests against the Vietnam War result in killing of four by National Guard troops at Kent State University, Ohio; 448 U.S. colleges and universities are closed or on strike.

1971 U.S. bombs Vietnam supply routes in Cambodia and conducts large-scale bombing raids against North Vietnam.

1972 Joan goes to North Vietnam. In the 1970s she tours Europe, Asia, and Latin America. Richard Nixon is reelected president of the U.S. in a near-record landslide.

1973 Joan works with Amnesty International setting up groups in the West Coast. Joan and David Harris are divorced. War in Vietnam ends.

1974 Joan becomes a member of the national advisory council of Amnesty International. The Federal Communications Commission establishes new guidelines to encourage the hiring of blacks and minorities. President Nixon is implicated in Watergate scandal. Nixon resigns and Vice-president Gerald R. Ford becomes president.

1975 Blacks in South Africa battle armed policemen as waves of rioting and violence against apartheid spread. James Earl Carter is elected president of the U.S.

1977 President Jimmy Carter grants amnesty to almost all the American draft evaders of the Vietnam War era.

1979 Joan appears in Germany. She goes on factfinding mission and launches campaign that raises over a million dollars for Southeast Asian refugee camps. Joan is the founder and president of Humanities/International Human Rights Commission.

1980 In the 1980s Joan reemerges as a singer and performer. Ronald Reagan is elected president in a landslide and is the first candidate since Franklin Roosevelt to defeat an incumbent.

1984 Joan joins "Conspiracy of Hope" concert tour. President Reagan is reelected.

1985 Joan Baez opens Live-Aid telecast to raise money to fight world hunger.

1988 George Bush is elected president of the U.S.

1990 Nelson Mandela, now 71 years old, is released from prison after serving over 27 years and says, "We must not allow fear to stand in our way."

INDEX- *Page numbers in boldface type indicate illustrations.*

Allman Brothers, 86

Amnesty International, 84-85

A & M Records, 81

And a Voice to Sing With (autobiography), 95

Baez, Alberto Vinicio "Popsy" (father), 13, 17-20, 21, 23, 26, 27, 29, 35, **47**, **52**

Baez, Joan Bridge (mother), 17-20, 21, 26, 27, 29, 35, **48**, 67-68

Baez, Joan Chandos: performance of, at Live Aid, 12-16; voice of, 15; as symbol, 17; relationship with father, 17-20; relationship with mother, 17-20; birth of, 19; move to Palo Alto, 19; move to Cornell, 19-20; prosperity of family, 19-20; early love of music, 20; religious experiences of, 20-21; move to California, 21; move to Iraq, 21-22; return to California, 22; ethnic background as problem for, 22-23; political interests of, 23; decision to train voice, 23-24; ukulele lessons for, 24; in school talent show, 24; amateur performances of, 25; reputation of, for speaking mind, 25; protest of, over air-raid drill, 25-26; first knowledge of Martin Luther King, Jr., 26; view of self, 26; move to Boston, 27; interest of, in pop music, 27-28; performances of, in coffeehouses, 28, 29; relationship with Michael New, 28-32, 34-35, 39-41; as drop-out from Boston University, 29; performance of, at Club Mt. Auburn 47, 29; performance of, at Gate of Horn, 31-32; performance at Folk Festival in Newport, R.I., 32-33; decision to make record, 34-35; move to California, 35-36; sales of first album, 36; involvement of, with Freedom Riders, 37-38; first concert tour of, 38; interest of, in nonviolence, 39; return to California, 39; impact of success on, 39; first meeting with Bob Dylan, 39-40; appearance of, at Miles College, 40-41; second concert tour of South, 40-41; meeting with Martin Luther King, Jr., 40; media attention on, 41-43; sessions with psychiatrist, 41; decision to say good-bye to Michael New, 43; third album of, 44; and Bob Dylan, 44-45; at King's "I Have a Dream" speech, 45-46; release of fourth album, 56; interest of, in Vietnam, 55-57; tax protest of, 57-58; relationship with Bob Dylan, 58-60; English tour with Dylan, 59-60; involvement of, in starting peace movement, 60-62; opening of Institute for the Study of Nonviolence, 61; concert tour of Japan, 63-64; as perfectionist, 64; money earned by, 64; concerts, of, 64; enjoyment of world pleasures by, 64-65; music of, 65-66; at Santa Rita Prison, 67-68; meeting with David Harris, 68; relationship with David Harris, 68-71, 95-96; marriage of, to David Harris, 69; and antidraft movement, 69-70; move to Struggle Mountain, 69; concert style of, 69-70; pregnancy of, 70, 71, 72; personality of, 70; at Woodstock, 72; birth of Gabriel, 73; split of, from David Harris, 73-74; as mother, 74, 95-96; writing of songs by, 74-75; split of, from Vanguard Records, 74; visit of, to Hanoi, 75-77; Milan concert of, 79-80; signing of, with A & M Records, 81; foreign tours of, 81-83; and Amnesty International, 84-85; and Bob Dylan, 86; as member of Rolling Thunder Tours, 86-87; signing of, with Portrait Records, 87; voice problems of, 87-88; German concert of, 88-90; continued interest of, in Vietnam, 91-93; visit to Southeast Asia, 93-94; formation of Humanitas, 94; reemergence as singer, 96-97; at Live Aid, 96; as member of "Conspiracy of Hope" concert tour, 96; publication of autobiography, 96; global music interests of, 96-97

Baez, Joan Chandos (albums of): *Diamonds and Rust*, 13, 85-86, 87; *Joan Baez*, 36; *Joan*, 65; *David's Album*, 72; *Any Day Now*, 72-73; *One Day at a Time*, 74; *Blessed Are . . .*, 74; *The First Ten Years*, 75; *Where Are You Now, My Son?*, 77; *Gracias a La Vida*, 82; *Speaking of Dreams*, 96-97

Baez, Joan Chandos (illustrations): **4**; performance of, **8**; with father, **47**, **52**; at age of three, **47**; at age of ten, **48**; with sisters Pauline and Mimi, **48**; with sisters, Pauline and Mimi, and Joan Sr. (mother), **48**; with Bob Dylan, **49**, **52**, **53**; with student demonstrators, **49**; in civil rights movement, **50**; with Martin Luther King, Jr., **50**; with husband, David Harris, **51**; with son Gabriel Earl, **51**; in Cambodia, **53**; in Hong Kong, **53**; at Newport Folk Festival, **54**; with Arlo Guthrie, **54**; with Judy Collins, and sister, Mimi, **54**; in concert for Amnesty International, **98**

Baez, Joan Chandos (songs sung by): "The Night They Drove Old Dixie Down," 13, 81; "Amazing Grace," 15; "We Are the World," 16; "Tom Dooley," 27, 28; "Fair and Tender Maidens," 28; "All My Trials," 28; "We Shall Overcome," 41, 72, 89; "Annabel Lee," 65; "The Dove," 65; "Children of Darkness," 65-66; "The Ghetto," 79; "We Shall Not Be Moved," 82-83; "Children and All That Jazz," 86; "Winds of the Old Days," 86; "Simple Twist of Fate," 86; "Diamonds and Rust," 87; "Where Have All the Flowers Gone?," 89; "Blowin' in the Wind," 89; "Children of the Eighties," 90; "I Love My Rooster," 94; "China," 96-97; "El Salvador," 97; "Hand to Mouth," 97

Baez, Mimi Margharita (sister). *See* Farina, Mimi Margharita Baez (sister)

Baez, Pauline Thalia (sister), 19, 27, **48**

"Band Aid," 10

Beatles, 32, 58, 65

Bernard, Robert, 88

Bond, Julian, 58

Bono, 10

Bowie, David, 11

Brel, Jacques, 65

Bridge, Meg, 18

British Airways, 12

Browne, Jackson, 80, 86

Chad Mitchell Trio, 31

civil rights movement, 37-38

Clapton, Eric, 11

Club Mt. Auburn 47, 29, 33, 96

coffeehouses, 28

Collins, Judy, **54**

Collins, Phil, 10

Committee for Solidarity with the American People, 75

Copeland, Greg, 97

Diem, Ngo Dihn, 55-56

Dire Straits, 11

Donovan, 65

Don't Look Back, 59

"Do They Know It's Christmas?," 10

Dylan, Bob, 39-40, 44-45, **49**, **52**, **53**, 58-60, 72-73, 86, 89

Ethiopia, civil war and famine in, 9-11

Farina, Mimi Margharita Baez (sister), 19, 27, 29, **48**, **54**, 65, 95

Farina, Richard, 65

Folk Festival in Newport, 32-33

Forrestal, Michael, 55, 56

Franco, Francisco, 82, 83

Freedom Riders, 37-38

Gabriel, Peter, 95

Gate of Horn, 31-32

Geldof, Bob, 9-11

Genesis, 88

Gibson, Bob, 32-33

106

Grossman, Albert, 31, 34
Guthrie, Arlo, **54**
Harris, David (husband), **51**, 68-71, 73-74, 95-96
Harris, Gabriel Earl (son), **51**, 95-96
Hendrix, Jimi, 72
HORIZON magazine, 42
Humanitas, 94
Ian, Janis, 86
Institute for the Study of Nonviolence, 61
Iraq, 21-22
Jackson, Michael, 16
Jagger, Mick, 11
JFK Stadium (Philadelphia), 12
Johnson, Don, 16
Johnson, Lyndon B., 46, 56, 60
Kennedy, John F., 37, 46, 55-56
King, Carole, 80
King, Martin Luther, Jr., 26, 39, 40, 45-46, **50**, 62
Kingston Trio, 27, 28, 32
Lennon, John, 32, 89
Limelighters, 31
"Live Aid" concert, 11-16, 95
McCartney, Paul, 32
Michael, George, 97
Miles College (Birmingham, Alabama), 40, 41
Mitchell, Joni, 80
New, Michael, 28-29, 34-35, 39-41, 43

Patterson, John, 37
Perkins Institute for the Blind, 34
Peter, Paul and Mary, 31-32
Portrait Records, 87
Quarry Men, 32
Resistance, The, 68
Richie, Lionel, 16
Rolling Thunder Tour, 86-87
Santa Rita Prison, 67-68
Schickele, Peter, 65-66
Simon, Paul, 65
Solomon, Maynard, 33-34, 75, 87
Solomon, Seymour, 33-34, 87
Spock, Benjamin, 58
Springsteen, Bruce, 44
Stevenson, Adlai, II, 58
Sting, 10, 95
Takasaki, 63-64
Taylor, James, 80
TIME, 42
U2, 10, 95
UNESCO (United Nations Educational, Scientific and Cultural Organization), 21
University of Baghdad, 21
Vanguard Records, 34, 75, 81, 87
Wembly Stadium (London), 11-12
Who, The, 72
Wonder, Stevie, 86
Woodstock, 14
Zappa, Frank, 88

About the Author

Jeff Heller is a freelance writer who specializes in scientific and medical topics. Based in Cherry Hill, New Jersey, Jeff writes feature articles, sales brochures, and scripts for videotape and multi-image presentations.

A music fan, Jeff has followed the career of Joan Baez for many years. He saw Ms. Baez perform at both Woodstock in 1967 and Live Aid in 1985.